A SUPPLEMENT TO
NOTAE LATINAE

A SUPPLEMENT TO
NOTAE LATINAE

(Abbreviations in Latin MSS. of
850 to 1050 A.D.)

BY

DORIS BAINS

Sub-librarian of Bedford College
(University of London)

With a Foreword by

W. M. LINDSAY, F.B.A.

CAMBRIDGE
AT THE UNIVERSITY PRESS
1936

CAMBRIDGE UNIVERSITY PRESS
Cambridge, New York, Melbourne, Madrid, Cape Town,
Singapore, São Paulo, Delhi, Mexico City

Cambridge University Press
The Edinburgh Building, Cambridge CB2 8RU, UK

Published in the United States of America by Cambridge University Press, New York

www.cambridge.org
Information on this title: www.cambridge.org/9781107684829

© Cambridge University Press 1936

First published 1936
First paperback edition 2013

A catalogue record for this publication is available from the British Library

ISBN 978-1-107-68482-9 Paperback

FOREWORD

After the publication of my 'Notae Latinae' (Cambridge 1915), an account of abbreviation in Latin manuscripts of the early minuscule period (c. 700–850), I began to collect the abbreviation-symbols of the two following centuries (850–1050), especially from manuscripts whose date could be determined with certainty. My growing deafness made continental travel difficult and prevented me from completing the collection. However Miss Bains, with the help of the Notcutt Travelling Scholarship, has managed to complete it and to embody the collected material in book-form. Her readers will not blame her for having now and then, where it seemed suitable, included some symbols of a slightly later date. The twelfth century, as Freeman says, was a great new birth of learning and science everywhere. It brought with it a new wave of abbreviation-symbols, but many of these shew themselves in the second half of the eleventh century; so that the year 1050, although the right limit for her book, is a limit that should not be too rigidly enforced.

In Continental script, that is to say the script of all parts of the continent of Europe except Spain (Visigothic script) and the southern half of Italy (Beneventan script), the Caroline type of writing introduced by Charlemagne and his successor, Louis the Pious, had assumed universal dominance. This type did not much favour the use of symbols in place of the fully written word. In Insular script (that is to say the script of Ireland, Wales and England) there is far more abbreviation, as will be seen from the statistics in the following pages. And Caroline writing did not change to any great extent until the end of the tenth century, so that it is often difficult to assign a manuscript with certainty to the tenth rather than to the ninth century. The famous manuscript of Cicero de Oratore in the Harleian Collection at the British Museum had been assigned by experts to the tenth century till Prof. Beeson, who has now published it in facsimile ('Lupus of Ferrières as Scribe and Critic,' Cambridge, Mass. 1930), proved that it was written by Servatus Lupus, abbot of Ferrières, 840–862. And the infrequency of abbreviation leaves us at a loss for clues to dating. Perhaps we may say that, as the ninth century passes into the tenth, we may expect to find in Continental script:

(1) For *prae* not merely p̄ but this symbol (or the mere letter *p*) with the ligature of *a* and *e* appended in cedilla form or with an *a* (often open *a*) written above.

(2) For *quae* similarly the cedilla appended.

And from the middle of the ninth century:

(3) *gloria* and *gratia* are abbreviated to glā, grā not merely (as before) in Italy and Spain, but everywhere.

(4) A great increase of the apostrophe (later an almost circular flourish like the number 9) to symbolize final *us* after any letter whatsoever.

(5) In the abbreviation of *frater* the symbol frēm is used for 'fratrem,' while frm̄ is reserved for 'fratrum.'

(6) *Christus, Iesus* and even *Spiritus* tend to substitute the Greek form of *s* for the Latin, xpc̄, ihc̄, spc̄.

In the eleventh century:

(7) *gentes* begins to be abbreviated (gs̄); but the abbreviation of *genus* (gr̄is 'generis,' etc.) is rather later.

But we have no clue so infallible (or so nearly infallible) as the symbolism of the final syllable *tur*, a clue which enables us to assign a manuscript to the earlier part of the ninth century. In 'Notae Latinae,' p. 376, statistics are provided which shew that t' denotes *tur* for that part, but later is replaced by t² (similarly m² comes into use for *mur*) while t' comes to be reserved for *tus*. In my 'Palaeographia Latina,' III, 13, I have added to these statistics and said: 'The evidence seems to me quite overwhelming; and if anyone pleads that a transcript may occasionally reproduce its exemplar's symbols, I reply: Not this symbol; for t' came to denote *tus* instead of *tur*, and the transcriber would feel the necessity for distinction.' All the leading palaeographers, so far as I know, have recognized this rule, although Prof. Lehmann rightly warns us that, since t' continued to denote *tur* to late times in Insular script, we may expect to find it abnormally persistent in scriptoriums under Insular influence. Every rule has exceptions (some I have mentioned in 'Palaeographia Latina,' v, 29, 35 and 36), but this rule of the symbolism of *tur* remains a rule for all that. It has been strikingly vindicated by Miss Bains ('Classical Review,' XLVI, 153).

The famous pictured manuscript of Terence in the Vatican Library
(*C*) has recently been published in facsimile (Leipzig 1929), and
Prof. Jachmann has stated in the preface that the scribe used t² as
the symbol of *tur*. Two years later Morey and Jones ('The
Miniatures in the MSS. of Terence: Text,' Princeton 1931) proved
that *C* was written at Corbie before the foundation of Corvey
(Corbeia Nova) in 822. How could this early date be reconciled
with the use of t² for *tur*? Miss Bains examined the manuscript
at Rome and found that the symbol which the scribe had actually
used was t', but that this had been altered (usually, not always) to
t² at some later time. After the publication of his 'Scholia in
Juvenalem Vetustiora' (Teubner 1931) Prof. Wessner told me that
in the Aarau fragment (Schedae Arovienses) the symbol of *tur*
was t', not t². His dating 'tenth century' is therefore wrong, and
possibly the manuscript to which the fragment belonged was
actually the missing archetype.

In Insular script these abbreviation-symbols give a clue to
dating manuscripts of our two centuries:

(1) The distinction of the symbols for the various parts of the
pronouns *hic* and *qui* becomes more and more blurred. Statistics
are given by Miss Bains. And h̄ comes into use as the Irish
symbol of *hic*.

(2) *caelum* finds a symbol (clm̄) in Irish and Welsh writing
from the tenth century onwards.

(3) Similarly *caput* 'head' (cp̄).

(4) Similarly the syllable *for* (f̄).

(5) Similarly *usque* (us̄).

(6) Rather later than our period Irish and Welsh scribes take
to writing *ut* with the *t* suprascript over *u* (generally in *v*-shape),
although this can hardly be called an abbreviation.

Of Beneventan script it seems unnecessary to speak. The Oxford
Reader in Palaeography, Dr E. A. Lowe (formerly Loew), has in
his two books, 'Beneventan Script' and the larger 'Scriptura
Beneventana,' supplied so full and so clear details that the dating
of South Italian MSS. has become easy for everyone.

He has also (in the Sitzungsberichte of the Bavarian Academy
of 1910, 'Studia Palaeographica') enabled us to date Visigothic
manuscripts. He says (p. 78) of the practice of distinguishing the

assibilated pronunciation of *ti* by joining to *t* an undotted *j*: 'The distinction is never found in MSS. which are indisputably of the eighth or early ninth century; the distinction is invariably made in the more recent MSS., beginning (to use the safest limits) with the second half of the tenth century and extending to the twelfth, i.e. as long as the script lasts; certain MSS. written between the two periods indicated show a wavering in usage, one scribe making the distinction and another not: or one scribe making it in some cases and not in others.'

I conclude with:

CORRECTIONS OF 'NOTAE LATINAE'

p. xi. On Cologne MSS. see now L. W. Jones 'The Script of Cologne from Hildebald to Hermann' (Cambridge, Mass. 1932). On Corbie MSS., Dobiache-Rojdestvensky 'Histoire de l'Atelier Graphique de Corbie de 651 à 830, reflétée dans les manuscrits de Leningrad' (Leningrad 1934). On Lorsch MSS., my article in 'Palaeographia Latina,' III, 1 (1924). On Lyons MSS., E. A. Lowe 'Codices Lugdunenses Antiquissimi' (Lyons 1924); S. Tafel in my 'Palaeographia Latina,' II, 66 (1923), and IV, 40 (1925). On Mayence MSS., the articles by Lehmann and me in 'Palaeographia Latina,' IV, 15 (1925). On Tours MSS., Rand 'A Survey of the Manuscripts of Tours' Vol. I Text, Vol. II Plates (Cambridge, Mass. 1929); Rand 'The Earliest Book of Tours' (Cambridge, Mass. 1934). On Verona MSS., Carusi and Lindsay 'Monumenta Palaeographica Veronensia' (Rome 1929 sqq.). On all MSS. earlier than 800, Lowe 'Codices Latini Antiquiores' (Oxford 1934 sqq.).

p. xiii. Mountford 'The Scholia Bembina' (Liverpool 1934) gives a full and accurate list of the ancient Notae in the Codex Bembinus of Terence.

p. xiv. Rand in 'Speculum,' II, 160 (1927), gives a list of ancient Notae transcribed from an uncial exemplar in a Tours manuscript (No. 286) of Augustinus de Musica. This confirms the theory that ancient Notae were used not merely in legal manuscripts but in all of a technical nature (on Music, on Grammar, on Rhetoric, etc.).

p. 4. On medieval lists of ancient Notae see now Lehmann 'Sammlungen und Erörterungen lateinischer Abkürzungen in Altertum und Mittelalter' in the Publications of the Bavarian Academy (Munich 1929); also his 'Mitteilungen aus Handschriften,' IV, 18, in the Proceedings of the Bavarian Academy (Munich 1933).

p. 5 top line: Oxford Jun. (not 'Douce') 25.

p. 7. In the Plautus line: errans (not 'absens').

p. 8 read: We may guess that it stood in the archetype (presumably a North Italian MS.) of our, etc. And omit: The guess...(see below on 'est,' 'enim,' 'con').

p. 10. The symbol ap' for 'apud' is found also in a Micy MS. of the middle of the ninth century, Paris 1862 (on f. 52ʳ 'apud hebreos'); in a MS. of unknown provenance, written in France in the year 813, Paris 2796 (e.g. on f. 80ᵛ more than once); in a Péronne (?) MS. of 'beg. 9 cent.,' Paris 13026.

p. 16. The Maihingen Gospels come from Echternach rather than Metz. Also p. 29.

p. 18 § 14: S. Vincenzo al Volturno (not 'near Benevento').

p. 19 to the Trèves MSS. add: Trèves 118, ff. 313–392 (bef. 847) aut. Of the St Amand MSS. the first is Paris 1603.

p. 20 to the second paragraph add: Paris 9517 (Beauvais, not after 840), aut. to the Fleury MSS. add: Vat. Reg. 846 (Orléans, bef. 814), aut. to the Lyons MSS.: Lyons 378 and Autun 5 (both of 840–852), aut.

p. 24 mid.: Paris Baluze 270, foll. 132–148 [Caroline (not 'Italian').

p. 27 § 21 add: Paris 13026 (Péronne?, "9 cent.") has cap' for 'caput,' ap' for 'apud.'

p. 30 § 24 add: Paris 13026 ("9 cent."), with cet, cētr, ctr, may come from Péronne.

p. 33 § 28 add: An early cursive marginal adscript of the uncial Leningrad Q ɪ 7–8 has cont nestorium.

p. 34 after § 31 add: **contradico** (see chap. ɪɪɪ).

p. 35 top: h' for 'huius' is one of the ancient Notae in Tours 286 Augustinus de Musica.

p. 37 to the second paragraph add: Vat. Pal. 177 (Lorsch, "beg. 9 cent.") on f. 54ʳ 'in mare huius saeculi.'

p. 38 top add: Prof. Souter tells me that Zürich Cantonsbibl. Rheinau lxxii ("10 cent.") Sedulii Collectaneum in Epp. S. Pauli has many examples of 'contra' corrected rightly to 'eius.' Cf. Hessels 'Leiden Glossary,' s.v. Agrippa, 'eius natura' for 'contra naturam.'

§ 35 end: London Add. 11880 (Bavaria?, "9 cent.") on f. 109ᵛ hs for 'huius.' Prof. Souter tells me that in a Reichenau MS., Carlsruhe Reich. 119 ("beg. 9 cent.") es twice appears for 'eius' (by analogy of cs 'cuius,' hs 'huius').

§ 36: Schwenke in 'Philologus' of 1888 says that eɪ 'eius' has been often mistaken for 'enim.'

p. 39 near foot: written in "767" (not "743").

p. 41 last line add: It has been mistaken for 'si' by the Vienna editors of 'Monumenta Palaeographica Vindobonensia' in an occurrence in Vienna 16.

p. 46 § 42: dc 'dicit' is used by one of the scribes of Paris 13026 (Péronne?, "9 cent."), e.g. on f. 139ᵛ.

p. 63 middle: the first form of ancient Nota appears in the Codex Bembinus of Terence in the scholium on Ad. 377.

p. 73 § 75 end: ē 'est' appears also, but rarely, in the half-uncial Vat. Reg. 1024.

p. 77 near foot: et 'etiam' in the half-uncial Cambrai 441 on f. 66ʳ 'vel etiam in ipsa adulescentia.'

p. 102 after § 112 add: **haeret.** De Bruyne in my 'Palaeographia Latina,' v, 48, and vi, 67, cites from MSS. of Biblical Commentaries the symbol hēt which indicates that one passage is related to another.

p. 110 middle: adō 'adeo' also in the Visigothic Leyden Voss. F 111. In a Lorsch MS., Vat. Pal. 1773 ("beg. 9 cent.") iđ 'ideo' ('Errantem lunam: aut incertam aut *ideo* ait quia inter planetas habetur'). In a Beauvais MS., Paris 9517 (not after 840) Clementis Recognitiones. on. f. 59ᵛ idō 'ideo.'

p. 114 **Iohannes**: see chap. ii, § 7 (not 'chap. iii').

p. 116 foot: In a Lorsch MS., Vat. Pal. 1773 Liber Glossarum ("beg. 9 cent."), on f. 170ᵛ 'in regnorum Ib' (expanded by a later corrector to 'libro').

p. 128 § 156: In Vat. Reg. 1997 (Chieti, "8–9 cent.") miša and mišm.

p. 150 (Irish): Traube, 'Nomina Sacra,' p. 217 says 'St Gallen 908 hat in der schönen wohl irischen Halb-Unciale die auf S. 79 beginnt, öfters dn̄m nr̄m. Dies dürfte eines der ältesten insularen Beispiele sein.'

p. 151 before third line: Paris 8901 + Toulouse 364 (Albi, bet. 660 and 666) dn̄m n̄m (once).

p. 152 § 193: St Gall 1395 (6ᶜ), p. 427 Irish Half-uncial Fragment of Litany, 'patribus nr̄s.' In the Stowe Missal (of 792–812) once (f. 40ᵛ) nr̄s 'nostris' and once (f. 17ʳ) nš 'nostris.'

p. 154 § 195: Dr Lowe adds (in a letter) Vienna 563 nša (f. 172ᵛ); Paris 13246 Bobbio Missal nše (f. 181ʳ), nšis (f. 284ʳ), ušm (f. 141ʳ).

p. 155 § 197: Paris 17227 (Tours, bef. 834) nr̄t, ur̄t.

p. 156 § 198 read: In Vat. Reg. 1997 (Chieti, "beg. 9 cent.") on f. 136ʳ redemptor nēr, and often (with nr̄i, sometimes ñi).

§ 199: Prof. Souter tells me of nōri (thrice) and uēri (twice) in Paris 653.

p. 157 after § 200: **num** (see the Syllable-symbol 'um').

p. 172 last line read: qualified by the occurrence of ōis, ōi, ōes, ōium, ōibus, ōe, ōia among the ancient Notae in Tours 286 Augustinus de Musica and by, etc.

p. 173 first line: Schiaparelli 'Il Codice CCCCXC della Biblioteca Capitolare di Lucca' (Rome 1924) finds Insular influence at the Lucca scriptorium.

p. 184. Prof. A. C. Clark in a review says that in Oxford Laud. misc. 135 (Würzburg, of 842–855) the first hand regularly writes 'pro' for 'per' (e.g. 'proseverat') and the corrector substitutes 'per' (e.g. on f. 17ᵛ thrice, on f. 18ᵛ five times).

p. 206 second last line: Vat. Reg. 846 (Orléans, bef. 814) 'qua' (with open *a*).

p. 219 second last line read: frequent in the early cursive of the Avitus papyrus (Paris 8913–4), according to Peiper, and in, etc.

p. 241 last line add: the Wigbald Gospels.

p. 252 § 314 (1): qš 'quis' in the Stowe Missal (along with qđ 'quid').

p. 257 to the Lorsch MSS. add: in Vat. Pal. 177 ("beg. 9 cent.") only the first of the scribes uses the Insular symbol, and a corrector has regularly altered it to q̄d.

p. 259 middle: Vat. Reg. 1997 (Chieti, "beg. 9 cent.") q̄ūd more often than qđ.

p. 266 § 335 add: The suspension from which this contraction is derived appears in the cursive marginalia of an uncial MS. 'ex arca Bobuleni' (abbot of Bobbio c. 640), Vat. lat. 5758 on p. 146 'quñ ipse liberavit nos.'

p. 275 before § 349: **sacerdos** (see §421 and chap. III).

p. 279 second line read: the scholia of the Bembine Terence use scil. The first of, etc.

    seventh line read: A third sī is fairly, etc.

p. 284 fourth line read: also ·s· (which occasionally denotes 'sic') while s̄ denotes 'sunt.'

p. 285 to the Swiss MSS. add: Geneva 50 Bede (of 830) on f. 57ᵛ.

    sententia read: (see 'satis' and chap. III).

p. 296 to the Lyons MSS. add: Lyons 378 (of 840–852) s̄.

p. 299 § 384: Keil ('Gramm. lat.' VI, 225, ad v. 10) cites from Vienna 16 (Bobbio, "c. 700") 's̄ scriptorum.'

p. 311 top: delete the statements about the Bembine scholia.

    second last line add: frequently in Vat. Reg. 846 Iuristica (Orléans, bef. 814).

p. 328 before (1) DE, add: but a MS. may be mentioned in which (as in Cassel theol. Q 10) the 'e' symbol is wonderfully frequent, Vat. Reg. 846 Iuristica (Orléans, bef. 814), e.g. 'de,' 'lege,' 'praecepimus,' '-ne,' '-re' (r̄ denotes '-re,' not '-runt'), 'clericorum,' 'naturale,' cedr̄ 'cedere,' etc.

p. 357 foot: A curious parallel to ḡ 'gre' is f̄ 'fre' of St Gall 912 (twice in 'frequenter,' p. 126, p. 235).

p. 359 second last line read: the 'um' of 'spinosum.'

p. 372 § 468: Prof. Walters tells me that t' for 'tur' appears in the Puteanus Livy (23, 48, 9 'staretur'; 23, 48, 5 'sumatur').

p. 423 26ᵃ. **contradico.** In rhetorical works often c̄d (e.g. Cologne 166 'contradicit,' etc.).

p. 453 106 delete: 'This seems...Salzburg.' Prof. L. W. Jones ('Speculum,' IV, 27) has proved that this is a Cologne, not a Tours, MS. So correct all ascriptions of Cologne 106 to Tours.

p. 454 DUBLIN, Ir. Acad., St Columba's Psalter, read: The tradition that Columba was the scribe seems correct. See Lawlor ('Proceedings Irish Academy,' Dublin 1916), with a full list of the symbols.

p. 459 LEYDEN 67 F: written probably at Amiens (Lowe 'Codices Latini Antiquiores,' no. 131).

p. 461 Utrecht Psalter: formerly Cotton Claud. C vii, now in Utrecht University Library.

p. 463 LYONS add: 378 (449) Bede on Book of Kings (given by bp. Amolus, 840–852). Among the abbreviations are: auꞇ 'autem'; ff 'fratres' (no other symbol of any case); 'gloria' and 'gratia' are written in full; ms̄ 'meus'; om̄is, om̄s, om̄a; q̇ 'qui' (f. 67ʳ 'quibus'); q̄ 'quae' (f. 18ᵛ); qm̄ 'quoniam' (very frequent); scl̄i 'saeculi'; secđm 'secundum'; s̄ 'sunt'; ul and (by one scribe) ᴉ 'vel'; x̄ '-xit,' đ '-dit'; r̄ 'runt'; t² 'tur.'

    MADRID. Tol. 2, 1 read: "saec. x med." (not 'saec. viii ex.'). See Anspach "Taionis et Isidori" (Madrid 1930), p. 141.

p. 471 Laud. Misc. 124 read: (written at Würzburg, 842–855).

p. 472 2440 read: (part of 1938 [Bourges, "saec. ix post."]).

p. 475 12048 The Sacramentary of Gellone, read: Wilmart ('Revue Béné-dictine,' xLII, 210) corrects the prevalent theory of its origin and shews that the same hand wrote ff. 6–9 of Cambrai 282 (300) Augustinus de Trinitate.

p. 478 before 491 delete: 'the booty of Gustavus Adolphus.'

p. 480 Pal. 493 read: Missale Gallicanum vetus (not 'Gelasianum').

p. 482 ROME, Arch. Vat. Capit. 138, add: There is a less famous MS. of the Liber Diurnus at Milan, Ambros. I 2 sup. (from Bobbio, "saec. ix post.").

ROME, Bibl. Casan. B iv 18, read: part i Alcuin de Trinitate; Treatises on Computus, etc....in 811–812) 'Munus hoc exiguum praeclaro, etc.'

p. 490 33 read: de Agone Christiano (not 'Christi').

p. 499 Anglosaxon column, *etiam* read: et̄ (rare).

p. 500 Anglosaxon column, *quem* read: q̄m (rare).

W. M. LINDSAY

CONTENTS

LIST OF WORD-SYMBOLS

	PAGE		PAGE
anima, animal, animus	1	ideo	20
ante	1	id est	20
apostolus	1	Iesus (see 'Christus')	20
apud	2	igitur (see 'ergo')	20
aut	2	in (see the Letter-symbol 'n')	20
autem	3	inter	20
bene	5	item	20
caelum	5	loquitur	20
caput	5	mater (see 'frater')	20
cetera, reliqua	6	meus, suus, tuus	21
Christus, Iesus, Spiritus	6	mihi, tibi	21
civitas	7	misericordia	22
contra	7	modo	23
cuius, eius, huius	7	nam	23
cum	9	nihil	23
dico, etc.	9	nisi	23
eius (see 'cuius').	12	nobis, vobis	24
enim	12	nomen	24
episcopus (see 'Christus')	12	non	25
epistula	12	noster, vester	25
ergo, igitur	12	numerus	27
est, esse	13	nunc, tunc	27
et	15	omnino (see 'omnis')	27
etiam	15	omnipotens.	27
facio	15	omnis, omnino	27
famulus	15	pater (see 'frater')	29
filius	16	per, prae, pro	29
flagellum	16	populus	30
fortis	16	post	31
frater, mater, pater	16	potest (see also 'est')	31
gens	17	prae (see 'per')	32
genus	18	praeter	32
gloria, gratia	18	pro (see 'per')	32
habeo, etc.	18	proprius	32
hic, haec, hoc, hunc. (For 'huius'		propter	32
see 'cuius') .	19	qua, quo	33
homo	19	quae	33
idem	19	quaeritur	34

	PAGE		PAGE
quaesumus	34	sequitur	45
quam	35	sicut	46
quando	35	similiter	46
quantus	36	sine	46
quare	36	sive	46
quasi	36	Spiritus	47
que	36	sunt	47
quem	36	super	48
qui	37	supra	48
quia	38	suprascriptus	48
quibus	38	suus (see 'meus')	48
quid	38	tamen	48
quippe	39	tantum	48
quis	39	tempore, etc.	48
quo (see 'qua')	39	ter	49
quod	39	tibi (see 'mihi')	49
quomodo	39	trans	49
quoniam	40	tunc (see 'nunc')	49
quoque	41	tuus (see 'meus')	49
quot	41	vel	49
reliqua (see 'cetera')	41	vero	50
res	42	vesper	51
respondeo, etc.	42	vester (see 'noster')	51
saeculum	42	vobis (see 'nobis')	51
scilicet	43	unde	51
secundum	43	usque	51
sed	45	ut	51

LIST OF SYLLABLE- AND LETTER-SYMBOLS

	PAGE		PAGE
con-	52	or	58
-e	52	ra, re, ri	58
-em	52	-s	59
en	53	ul	60
er	53	-um	60
-is	55	-unt	61
-it	55	ur	62
m	56	-us	64
n	57		

	PAGE
DESCRIPTION OF MANUSCRIPTS	68

LIST OF WORD-SYMBOLS

(MSS. later than 1050 *are enclosed in square brackets)*

anima, animal, animus. The abbreviation of these words is perhaps later than our period, e.g.: am̄s, am̄a, am̄us, aı̄o, am̄i, am̄al, āal, am̄adverto in [Leyden 118] Cicero de Nat. Deorum, etc. (written at Monte Cassino in the abbacy of Desiderius), and aı̄e on folio 37 v of Brit. Mus., Cotton Vesp. A VIII, which is a later addition, probably early twelfth century. Lowe (Loew) 'Beneventan Script' (p. 175) however seems to claim it for Beneventan script as early as the first half of the eleventh century. He says: "In MSS. of the eleventh century the typically Beneventan form of the contraction is already established. This form is am̄a. Toward the end of the century āā is found by the side of am̄a. At about the same time the Insular and Continental form aı̄a is introduced, but used sparingly." He ascribes am̄s 'animus' to "saec. xi ex."

ante. The añ symbol is still extensively used by Irish and Welsh scribes. In the Continental script of St Gall 260 (of 860–867) the abbreviation-stroke stands to the right of the *n*. An Anglosaxon example of añ is Boulogne 90 Amalarius; a Breton is Cambridge, Corp. Christi 192 Amalarius (written in Continental minuscule at Landevenec in the year 952).

Of Irish MSS. may be mentioned: the **Macdurnan** Gospels at Lambeth (about the year 900); the Southampton Psalter at St John's, Cambridge ("saec. x–xi"); Laon 122bis, fly-leaves ("saec. x"); Berne 363 (of 855–869).

Of Welsh: the Martianus Capella ("saec. ix–x") and the [Augustine de Trinitate] (of 1085-1091) at Corp. Christi, Cambridge; the [Ricemarch Psalter] of Trin. Coll., Dublin (of 1085–1091); the marginalia ("saec. ix–x") in Cambridge Ff IV 32.

Lowe (Loew) 'Beneventan Script' (p. 176) assigns the symbol to Beneventan script of "saec. xi."

apostolus. The great variety of symbolism mentioned in 'Notae Latinae' continues throughout our period. But the scribe of Laon 136 (of 847–903) brings in the Irish symbol (p̊) of 'post' by writing ap̊li instead of apli. Visigothic scribes follow their usual practice of omitting vowels, e.g. apstĭs, apstĭus, apsĭi in the Gregory's Moralia (of the year 914), and apstĭs, apsĭs, aptĭs in the Smaragdus (of 945) at the Rylands Library, Manchester; apstĭi, apsĭi in Madrid, Bibl. Nac. 10007 (of 902); apstĭm, apsĭm in Madrid, Bibl. Acad. Hist. 24–25 (of 946); apsĭs, apstĭm in Manchester, Rylands 89; and apsĭlorum in Brit. Mus., Add. 25600.

apud. The ancient Nota a͞p continues to be used by Irish, Welsh and Breton scribes both at home and on the Continent. The same MSS. may be cited as were cited for the abbreviation of 'ante,' e.g.:

(Irish) the Macdurnan Gospels at Lambeth (of c. 900); the Southampton Psalter of St John's, Cambridge; Berne 363 (of 855–869), etc.

(Welsh) the Martianus Capella of Corp. Christi, Cambridge, etc.

(Breton) Paris 3182 Canons (written by the scribe Madoc "saec. xi"); Brit. Mus., Cotton Otho E xiii Canons ("saec. x"), etc.

In Anglosaxon script the occurrences of this symbol are still few, only one example of a home specimen (Brit. Mus., Cotton Vitell. C viii, of "saec. ix ex.") and one of a Continental (Boulogne 90, "saec. x") having been noted.

The symbol occurs also in such MSS. under Insular influence as: Laon 468 (of 841–903); Paris 1761 ("saec. ix post."); Cologne 113 Canons (before 1022).

The only other form of abbreviation is a͞pd, which occurs in [Leyden 118] Cicero de Nat. Deorum, etc. (written at Monte Cassino in the abbacy of Desiderius), etc. It is rather the conventional expression of suprascript *u* by a horizontal stroke than a genuine contraction.

aut. The ancient Nota ā continues to be used in Insular script and in Continental script written under Insular influence. No examples have been found in Anglosaxon MSS. of this period.

(Irish) the Macdurnan Gospels at Lambeth (c. 900); Cambridge, Corp. Christi 279 Canons (with Irish glosses, "saec. ix–x"); Laon 122bis, ff. 25-26 ("saec. x"); Berne 363.

(Welsh) the [Ricemarch Psalter] of Trin. Coll., Dublin (of 1085–1091); Cambridge, Corp. Christi 153 ("saec. ix") and [199] (of 1085–1091).

(Breton) Brit. Mus., Cotton Otho E xiii ("saec. x").

In Leyden 88 Martianus Capella (not in Irish script, but copied from an Irish exemplar) the symbol appears. And it is used in glossaries, such as Leyden 67 D ("saec. x").

autem. (I) The Insular h-symbol is the only abbreviation of 'autem' in such MSS. as: Berne 363 (Irish, 855–869); Lambeth 218 (Anglosaxon, "saec. ix"); Brit. Mus., Cotton Vitell. C VIII (Anglosaxon, "saec. ix ex."); Cassel theol. F 25 (Anglosaxon of Fulda, "saec. ix post."); Basel O IV 17 (Anglosaxon of Fulda, "saec. ix post."). And even later than our period in [Dublin, Trin. Coll. A IV 20] the Ricemarch Psalter (Welsh, of 1085–1091); [Cambridge, Corp. Christi 199] (Welsh, of 1085–1091); [Oxford, Bodl., Rawl. B 502] (Irish, of c. 1100).

It is found in conjunction with auṫ in such MSS. as: Boulogne 90 Amalarius (Anglosaxon, of "saec. x"); Brit. Mus., Cotton Otho E XIII (Breton, of "saec. x in."); Cambridge, Corp. Christi 307, part I (Anglosaxon, of "saec. ix–x").

With aū and auṫ in: Berne 207 (Brittany?, "saec. ix–x"); Berne 128 (of 1008–1029; usually aū).

With aṫ (a rarer Insular symbol) in: the Southampton Psalter of St John's Coll., Cambridge (Irish, of "saec. x–xi"); the Welsh Cambridge Ff IV 32 (saec. ix–x).

With aṫ and aū in: the Macdurnan Gospels of Lambeth (Irish, of c. 900).

With aṫ and auṫ in: the Insular portion of Oxford, Bodl. 572 ("saec. x"); Cambridge, Corp. Christi 153 (Welsh, "saec. ix").

The above statistics shew that the h-symbol is still the symbol in Insular script. Outside that province (including Breton, a branch of Cornish or South Welsh) it does not occur.

The ancient Nota aṫ persists likewise in Insular MSS. only. It is found with auṫ in: Frankfort, St Barthol. 32 (Anglosaxon of Fulda, "saec. ix post."), and with aū and auṫ in: Paris 1761, ff. 1–12ʳ ("saec. ix post.").

(II) The Continental symbols aū and auṫ. We find no quite clear definition of their use.

Only aū appears in Beneventan script (see Lowe [Loew] 'Beneventan Script,' p. 198), e.g.:

Glasgow, Hunter. V 3. 2 ("saec. x"); Paris 335 ("saec. ix–x"); Rome, Vitt. Eman., Sess. 56.

Both aū and auꞇ in the following MSS. from Switzerland: Brit. Mus., Add. 11852 (St Gall, before 883); St Gall 7 (of 872–883); St Gall 260 (of 860–867); St Gall 90 (of 860–867).

In the following from Germany: Épinal 78 (Murbach, "saec. x in."); Trèves, Stadtbibl. 170 ("saec. x"); Stuttgart H. B. VII 29 (of 1034–1046); Munich 13038 (of "saec. ix ex."); Munich 6262 (of 854–875; auꞇ only once). And also in: Brit. Mus., Harl. 3017 (Fleury, of 861–868); Oxford, Laud. lat. 26 (Brittany?, "saec. ix ex."); Autun 45 (auꞇ usual); Brussels 1370 (of 975–993); Rome, Vitt. Eman., Sess. 45 (of 1003–1035); Rome, Vitt. Eman., Sess. 44 (of 1003–1035; the second scribe uses aū only).

But auꞇ is the sole symbol in the following MSS. from Germany: Cologne 143 (of 985–999); Düsseldorf B 80 ("saec. ix–x"); Trèves, Dombibl. 136 ("saec. xi"); Trèves, Stadtbibl. 122 (of c. 883); Trèves, Stadtbibl. 169 ("saec. x ex.").

In the following from Switzerland: Berne 87 (of 1004); Berne 169 (of 1008–1089); Berne 236 (of 911); Berne 172 ("saec. x"); Berne 292 (Metz, of c. 1060).

In the following from Belgium and Holland: Brussels 10470–3 ("saec. x"); Hague 5 ("saec. ix ex."); Leyden 88 ("saec. ix ex."); Leyden 21 ("saec. ix post.").

In the following from France: Laon 122 and 136 and 265 and 464 and 468 (all of 847–903); Laon 97 and 428 (both of c. 883); Laon 444 (of 858–869); Autun 31 ("saec. x") and 15 and 22; St Omer 33bis ("saec. ix–x"); St Omer 765 (of 986–1007); Paris 12052 (Corbie, of 945–986); Orléans 79 ("saec. ix ex."); Valenciennes 195 (Anglosaxon, "saec. ix–x"); Paris 3182 (Breton, "saec. xi").

And also in: [Vienna 1247] (of 1079); Rome, Vitt. Eman., Sess. 71 (of 895–907); Cambridge Ee II 4 ("saec. x in."); Cambridge, Corp. Christi 279 ("saec. ix–x"); Brit. Mus., Add. 22820 (of 948–994); Brit. Mus., Cotton Vesp. B VI (ff. 1–103 of c. 848); Manchester, Rylands 98 ("saec. x ex.") and 7 ("saec. xi"); Lambeth 204 ("saec. x–xi," from Ely) and 427 ("saec. x–xi").

(III) The Spanish symbol aūm. The following Visigothic MSS. may be cited: Manchester, Rylands, Gregorii Moralia (of 914); Manchester, Rylands 104 (of 945; also aū) and 89 (of 949); Madrid, Bibl. Nac. 10007 (of 902) and 42 (not after 988); Madrid, Bibl.

Acad. Hist. 10067 (of 915) and 24 (of 917) and 25 (of 946); Brit. Mus., Add. 25600.

bene. Cross-barred *b* (ƀ) is still the Insular symbol. Irish and Welsh scribes use it freely, also Breton. Examples are: (Irish) the Macdurnan Gospels at Lambeth (c. 900); the Southampton Psalter of St John's Coll., Cambridge ("saec. x–xi"); Leyden 67 D (Continental Irish, "saec. x"). Also ƀignus, e.g. [Oxford, Bodl., Rawl. B 502] (c. 1100); Berne 363 (of 855–869). (Welsh) the [Ricemarch Psalter] of Trin. Coll., Dublin and [Cambridge, Corp. Christi 199] (both of 1085–1091); Cambridge Ff IV 32 ("saec. ix–x"); Cambridge, Corp. Christi 153 ("saec. ix–x").

(Breton) Brit. Mus., Cotton Otho E XIII ("saec. x"); Oxford, Laud. lat. 26 (Brittany?, "saec. ix ex.").

(Anglosaxon) Brit. Mus., Cotton Vitell. C VIII, ff. 86–90 ("saec. ix ex.").

(Cornish?) Oxford, Bodl. 572 ("saec. x."; also ƀne).

Its appearance in Cambridge Ee II 4 (Caroline minuscule, "saec. x in."), Leyden 88 ("saec. ix ex.") and Lambeth 204 ("saec. x–xi," from Ely) is due to Insular influence.

Confusion with the similar symbol used for the syllables 'bis' and 'ber' is not likely to occur in this common word.

caelum. A few instances of abbreviation of this word (a 'nomen sacrum' in Greek) occur in late MSS. by Irish and Welsh scribes. Thus the Southampton Psalter of St John's, Cambridge ("saec. x–xi") has clōs; [Oxford, Bodl., Rawl. B 502] (c. 1100) has clm̄, clī, clō; the Welsh MS. of 1085–1091 at Cambridge [Corp. Christi 199] has clī.

Is it really later than our period?

caput. The abbreviation of this word is late. In a Nonantola MS. at Rome, Vitt. Eman., Sess. 45 (of 1003–1035), the three-letter suspension cap̄ occurs. Similarly in the Beneventan script of [Leyden 118] ("saec. xi post.") both cap̄ and cap̄t, the latter probably a mere conventional expression of suprascript *u*. And two late Irish MSS., [Oxford, Bodl., Rawl. B 502] (c. 1100) and the [Book of Deer] at Cambridge, have the form cp̄, a syllabic suspension, possibly suggested by the Irish symbol of 'apud' or 'aput' ap̄.

cetera, reliqua. For 'cetera' cet̄ is still the commonest form
of abbreviation, e.g.: Brit. Mus., Add. 22820, ff. 1–50 (Cluny, of
948–994); Laon 50 (of 847–903); Autun 17ᴬ ("saec. ix–x"); Autun
15 ("saec. x–xi"; also cet̄r, c̄, ct̄); Brussels 10470–3 (also cet̄r);
Valenciennes 195 (Anglosaxon, "saec. ix–x"); Cassel theol. F 25
(Anglosaxon, "saec. ix post."); Frankfort, St Barthol. 32 (Anglosaxon, "saec. ix post."); Trèves, Stadtbibl. 122 (of 883); Munich
6262 (Freising, of 854–875); Berne 128 (of 1008–1029); Rome,
Vitt. Eman., Sess. 45 (Nonantola, of 1003–1035).

We find cet̄r̄ in the Trèves Cathedral Gospels of "saec. xi";
Lambeth 149 ff. 1–138 ("saec x," Anglosaxon) and 237 ff. 146–208
("saec. x"); cr̄a in Cambridge, Corp. Christi 192 (of 952); cr̄
in Boulogne 90 (Anglosaxon, "saec. x") and in Berne 167
(Fleury, "saec. ix–x"). And 'ceteri' is expressed by ct̄i in the
Beneventan script of [Leyden 118] (Monte Cassino, in abbacy of
Desiderius).

For 'reliqua' a great variety of capricious abbreviations occur in
the phrase 'et reliqua.' The commonest is rl̄, and is quite clearly
still the Insular symbol, e.g. in the following: Frankfort, St Barthol.
32 (Anglosaxon of Fulda, "saec. ix post."); Cassel theol. F 25
(Anglosaxon of Fulda, "saec. ix post."); Paris 3182 (Breton, "saec.
xi"); Leyden 67 D (Continental Irish, "saec. x"); Laon 468 (of
847–903); Épinal 78 (Murbach, "saec. x in."); Oxford, Bodl. 572
(Cornish?, "saec. x"); Cambridge Ff ɪv 32 (Welsh, "saec. ix–x");
Cambridge, St John's, the Southampton Psalter (Irish, "saec. x–xi");
Cambridge, Corp. Christi 279 (with Irish glosses, "saec. ix–x") and
192 (Insular, of 952) and 307 (Insular, "saec. ix–x").

But rel̄ is the form used in such MSS. as: Laon 50 (of 847–903);
Rome, Vitt. Eman., Sess. 45 (Nonantola, of 1003–1035); Manchester,
Rylands 104 (Visigothic, of 945).

To enumerate the variations would be tedious, e.g.:
rl̄, rel̄, rel̄q in Berne, 236 (of 911) and Stuttgart H. B. vɪɪ 29
(Constance, of 1034–1046).

rl̄, rel̄q, rl̄q, rel̄q̊ in Cologne 113 (of 999–1021).

Christus, Iesus, Spiritus. In 'Notae Latinae' (p. 403) the
variety xp̄c 'Christus' (with the Latin expression of the Greek
Sigma) is said not to have become current before 850 on the Continent, and (p. 407) ih̄c 'Iesus' to have gone hand in hand with

xp̄c. Here are examples from our period: St Omer 56 and 342bis; Düsseldorf D 1 and B 80; Stuttgart H. B. vii 29; Trèves, Dom. 136; Trèves, Stadtbibl. 169 (often xp̄c); Brit. Mus., Add. 11852 (by the first scribe) and 22820 (xp̄c on f. 17ᵛ, etc.); Brit. Mus., Cotton Titus D xxvii; Berne 292; Lambeth 204 and 431 (ff. 145–160). These forms are often or usually accompanied by the forms xp̄s, iħs.

Even 'Spiritus,' used as a 'nomen sacrum,' may be written sp̄c by a curious perversion. Examples are: Stuttgart H. B. vii 29; Berne 292 (sp̄c scs). Presumably the rare ep̄c 'episcopus' of Berne 292, etc., is to be referred to this analogy, and was not a syllabic suspension. Ep̄c and archiep̄c (archiepiscopus) are both frequent in a charter of Edward the Confessor of 1059.

civitas. In Berne 363, the famous Irish MS. of Horace, Virgil, etc., written by one of the circle of Sedulius in North Italy, the suspension civī is used for any case.

Similarly civv̄ in [Oxford, Bodl., Rawl. B 502] (of c. 1100).

contra. A reversed c (ɔ) was the Insular symbol of the syllable 'con.' For 'contra' this was transected by a horizontal stroke or else was doubled (ɔɔ). Both these Insular symbols of 'contra' are still used in our period in Insular script, e.g.: the first in Brit. Mus., Cotton Vitell. C viii, ff. 86–90 (Anglosaxon, "saec. ix ex."); the Southampton Psalter of St John's, Cambridge (Irish, "saec. x–xi"); Cambridge, Corp. Christi 153 (Welsh, "saec. ix, saec. x"). And the second, e.g.: Cambridge Ff iv 32 (Welsh, "saec. ix–x"); Leyden 67 D (Continental Irish, "saec. x").

The word can also be shortened by the use of a symbol of 'con,' either the Insular (ɔ) or the Continental (c̄). Or of a symbol of 'tra,' either the Insular (ť) on the superscription of a (usually in open form) over t. Or both syllables may be so treated.

cuius, eius, huius. Symbols for 'eius' are still far more common than for 'cuius' or 'huius.' The Insular symbol, a reversed e of uncial form, occurs in such Insular MSS. as: the Macdurnan Gospels of Lambeth; Lambeth 149 (ff. 1–138); the Southampton Psalter of St John's, Cambridge; the [Ricemarch Psalter] of Trin. Coll., Dublin; Brit. Mus., Cotton Vitell. C viii; Berne 363; Basel O iv 17; Frankfort, St Barthol. 32; Leyden 67 D; Laon 50;

Boulogne 90; Cassel theol. F 25. In the last MS. it is sometimes
found in its early form, with the tongue hanging down; and in
Boulogne 90 there is sometimes a redundant abbreviation-stroke
above.

The ancient Nota (e') seems not to have survived to 850, nor
has its Irish counterpart (ħ) for 'huius.' The more precise form of
the latter (hs̄) occurs in such Insular MSS. as: the Macdurnan
Gospels of Lambeth; Berne 363; Berne 207 (Fleury); Leyden
67 D and 88 (both under Irish influence); Brit. Mus., Cotton Otho
E xiii (Breton); Basel O iv 17 (Anglosaxon).

The similar form (cs̄) for 'cuius' occurs in such Insular MSS. as:

(Irish) Berne 363; Leyden 67 D and 88 (both under Irish influence),

(Welsh) [Dublin, Trin. Coll. A iv 20],

(Breton) Brit. Mus., Cotton Otho E xiii; Berne 167,

(Cornish?) Oxford, Bodl. 572,

(Anglosaxon) Brit. Mus., Cotton Vitell. C viii.

Thus these originally Irish forms have not penetrated into
Continental script, except when due to Insular influence. Nor
have they gained much footing in Anglosaxon manuscripts.

The normal Continental abbreviation (eī) of 'eius' occurs in such
MSS. as: Rome, Vitt. Eman., Sess. 45 (Nonantola, of 1003–1035);
Berne 169 (of 1001–1029); Berne 167 ("saec. ix–x"); Basel B i 6
("saec. x"); Basel B iv 12 (of 965–991; also the redundant form eī:).

The Beneventan variety, with the abbreviation-stroke descending
through the tail of the i, may be illustrated by: [Leyden 118]
(Monte Cassino, in abbacy of Desiderius); Paris 335; Glasgow
v 3. 2; Rome, Vitt. Eman., Sess. 56. It is also found in Autun 15
(Continental minuscule, of 997–1023), but is only used by the first
scribe, who affects a ligatured 'ei.' To express 'eius' he lengthens
the i of this ligature in the Beneventan fashion.

The Visigothic variety (eI with cross-stroke through the upper
part of the I) has (accidentally?) not been noted in MSS. of our
period.

All three words, 'cuius,' 'eius,' 'huius,' but especially 'eius,' may
be shortened by the use of the symbol for the final syllable 'us';
and this Syllable-symbol has different forms in Insular, Continental,
and Visigothic script. (See below, on Syllable-symbols.)

cum. The Insular symbol (c̄) of 'cum' denotes in Continental script the syllable 'con.' This Insular symbol appears in such Insular script (or under Insular influence) as: the Southampton Psalter of St John's, Cambridge (Irish, "saec. x–xi"); Berne 363 (Irish, of Sedulius' time); Leyden 88 (from an Irish exemplar); Cambridge Ff IV 32 (Welsh, "saec. ix–x"); [Cambridge, Corp. Christi 199] (Welsh, of 1085–1091); Brit. Mus., Cotton Otho E XIII (Breton, "saec. x"); Oxford, Bodl. 572 (Cornish ?, "saec. x"); Brit. Mus., Cotton Vitell. C VIII, ff. 86–90 (Anglosaxon, "saec. ix ex."). In the Macdurnan Gospels of Lambeth the symbol sometimes has the form of our capital *g* (G).

The syllable 'cum' is sometimes expressed by the preposition-symbol (see below, on Syllable-symbols, p. 61).

The symbols (nobc, vobc) of 'nobiscum, 'vobiscum' often shew the abbreviation-stroke to the right of the *b*, though not directly over the *c*, e.g. Berne 207 (Fleury, "saec. ix–x"), Munich 13038 (Ratisbon).

dicit, dixit. There is very little trace of the ancient Nota, the initial-letter suspension (*d* with a cross-stroke) in our period. It is, however, fairly common in two Visigothic manuscripts from S. Pedro de Cardeña, Manchester, Rylands 89 (of 949) and Brit. Mus., Add. 25600 (of 919). In both manuscripts the cross-stroke passes obliquely through the body of the letter, and neither contains any other *dixit* abbreviation. Berne 207 (Fleury, "saec. ix–x") has đ for 'dicuntur' on f. 29ʳ and the same symbol doubled for 'dixerunt' on f. 189ᵛ.

Turning to the two-letter syllable-suspensions of 'dicit' and 'dixit,' dc̄ and dx̄ respectively, we find the former, always a rare symbol, in Brit. Mus., Add. 24142 (Caroline minuscule, "saec. ix post."). The latter (dx̄), far more common, seems to be now confined to Insular script, e.g.: Brit. Mus., Cotton Vitell. C VIII (Anglosaxon, "saec. ix ex."); Cassel theol. F 25 (Anglosaxon of Fulda, "saec. ix post."); Valenciennes 195 (Anglosaxon, "saec. ix–x"; on f. 22ᵛ a corrector adds an *i* above the *d*); Oxford, Bodl. 572 (Cornish?, "saec. x"); Berne 363 (Irish, of Sedulius' time); the Macdurnan Gospels of Lambeth (Irish, of c. 900); the [Ricemarch Psalter] of Trin. Coll., Dublin (Welsh, of 1085–1091).

But a very common practice is to shorten 'dicit' and 'dixit' by use of the syllable-suspension of 'it' and to write dic̄ and dix̄ (see

below, on Syllable-symbols). The variety dix̄t 'dixit' appears in
Laon 50 (of 847–903).

The contraction dt̄ 'dicit' is frequent in Insular script, but not
confined to it, e.g.: the Macdurnan Gospels (Irish); Berne 363
(Irish); the [Ricemarch Psalter] (Welsh); Brit. Mus., Cotton Otho
E XIII (Breton); Oxford, Bodl. 572 (Cornish?); Paris 3182 (Breton,
"saec. xi"); Brit. Mus., Cotton Vitell. C VIII (Anglosaxon); Cassel
theol. F 25 (Anglosaxon of Fulda); Frankfort, St Barthol. 32 (Anglosaxon of Fulda); Lambeth 149, ff. 1–138 (Anglosaxon); Laon 50 (of
847–903); Cambridge, Corp. Christi 192 (of 952); Paris 1761;
Berne 167; Berne 207 (Fleury); Leyden 67 D and 88; Autun 17ᴬ
(d̄t). A variety (dīt) appears along with it in Lambeth 149 (f. 73ʳ),
Paris 3182 and Berne 167; also (alone) in Munich 6262 (of 854–
875) and 13038 (Ratisbon, "saec. ix ex.").

dicunt. Analogous to dt̄ 'dicit' is dn̄t 'dicunt,' a symbol fairly
common in our period. All our examples are from Insular (or Breton)
script: the Macdurnan Gospels (Irish); Leyden 67 D (under Irish
influence); Cambridge Ff IV 32 (Welsh); the [Ricemarch Psalter]
(Welsh); Paris 3182 (Breton, "saec. xi"); Berne 207 (Fleury,
"saec. ix–x"); Brit. Mus., Cotton Otho E XIII (Breton); Cambridge,
Corp. Christi 153 (Welsh).

dixerunt. Similarly in Cambridge, Corp. Christi 279 (with
Irish glosses, "saec. ix–x"), we find dx̄t for 'dixerunt.'

dicitur. The most widely used of all 'dico' abbreviations is dr̄
'dicitur.' It is so universal in Anglosaxon, Irish, Welsh, Breton, as
well as in Beneventan and Continental script, that examples are
unnecessary. It seems safe to say that any MS. shewing symbols
for any form of 'dico' (except those few that confine themselves to
shortening 'dicit' and 'dixit') will shew dr̄ 'dicitur.' The following
varieties (fairly frequent before our period) may be mentioned:

(1) dc̄r in Rome, Vitt. Eman., Sess. 45 (along with dr̄).

(2) dīr in Berne 167 (along with dr̄); St Gall 260; Trèves,
Stadtbibl. 170; Munich 13038.

To the dc̄t form, which appears thus in a MS. earlier than our
period, St Omer 15 ("saec. ix in."), is added the Syllable-symbol of
' ur' in Basel B IV 12 (of 905–991).

dicuntur. Analogous to dr̄ 'dicitur' is dn̄r 'dicuntur,' a symbol
fairly common in Insular and Continental script, e.g.: Brit. Mus.,

Cotton Vitell. C viii (Anglosaxon); Leyden 67 D (under Irish influence); Cambridge, Corp. Christi 153 (Welsh) and [199] (Welsh); Paris 3182 (Breton); Berne 207 (Fleury); Berne 87 (Luxeuil, of 1004); Rome, Vitt. Eman., Sess. 44 and 45 (of 1003–1035); Brit. Mus., Cotton Vesp. B vi (c. 848), ff. 1–103.

The variety dn̄tr (analogous to dn̄t 'dicunt') appears (along with dn̄r) in the above-mentioned Paris 3182.

dicens. The present participle shews various forms. The contraction (dc̄s), formed from the syllabic suspension (dc̄), is found only in Insular script, e.g.: the Macdurnan Gospels (Irish); [the Book of Deer] (Irish); Cambridge, Corp. Christi 153 (Welsh). The Macdurnan Gospels have an analogous plural, dc̄es 'dicentes,' also the suspension dicen̄ 'dicentes' and 'dicentem.'

A more precise form (dc̄ns), which in the early Book of Mulling denotes 'dicentes,' is found in Cassel theol. F 25 (Anglosaxon of Fulda, "saec. ix post."); [Oxford, Bodl., Rawl. B 502] (Irish, of c. 1100); [Cambridge, Corp. Christi 199] (Welsh, of 1085–1091; dcn̄te 'dicente').

The form dic̄s, like its counterpart dic̄ 'dicit,' occurs mainly in Continental script, e.g.: Rome, Vitt. Eman., Sess. 44 and 45 (of 1003–1035; Autun 31 and 45; St Gall 7; Berne 236; Berne 363 (Irish); Munich 13038; Manchester, Rylands 7.

The dicn̄s of Boulogne 90 (Anglosaxon) and Brit. Mus., Add. 11852 (St Gall, before 883) may also be mentioned. And still another form (dn̄s) occurs in Brit. Mus., Add. 24142 ("saec. ix post."); it is of course normally a symbol of 'Dominus.'

dicere. The sole symbol is still dr̄e, confined to Insular script, e.g. Berne 363 (Irish; dr̄et 'diceret'); the Macdurnan Gospels (Irish); Oxford, Bodl. 572 (Cornish?); Cambridge, Corp. Christi 153 (dr̄e 'dicere' and dr̄et 'diceret') and [199] (both Welsh).

dicimus. Another contraction (dm̄s) is likewise Insular, e.g. Berne 363 (Irish); Berne 167 (with Breton glosses); Berne 207 (Fleury); Oxford, Bodl. 572 (Cornish?); Cambridge, Corp. Christi 153 (Welsh).

diximus. Analogous is dxm̄s in Brit. Mus., Cotton Otho E xiii (Breton); Berne 207 (Fleury).

dictum. The suspension (dic̄) seems to be disappearing in our period, the only example noted being in Berne 363 (Irish). On

f. 10ᵛ of Leyden 67 D ('brancos a raucedine pulmonum dic') it may mean 'dicitur,' a glossarial usage.

The contraction (dc̄m) occurs in such Insular MSS. as: the two Welsh MSS., Cambridge, Corp. Christi 153 (also dc̄a 'dicta') and [199] (also dc̄i 'dicti'); the late Irish MSS., [Oxford, Bodl., Rawl. B 502] (dc̄i 'dicti') and the [Book of Deer]. Spanish script still admits no 'dico' abbreviation. Elsewhere we can see that the symbols have reached a much more definitive stage in our period. Irish and occasionally Beneventan script still cling to an earlier form, but elsewhere the tendency to establish more precise forms has left very little room for confusion in transcribing.

eius (see 'cuius').

enim. The H-symbol is universal in Insular script (and Breton). Examples need not be given. It is not unknown in Continental script, but most often found at Insular centres. Examples are: St Omer 765; Laon 50 and 468; Cologne 143; Munich 6262 (rare) and 13038 (supra-linear, once); Paris 1761 (N. Italy?).

episcopus (see 'Christus').

epistula. The common Continental symbol (epła) is ubiquitous, e.g.: Cologne 143; Cambridge Ee II 4; Boulogne 90 (Anglosaxon); Cambridge, Corp. Christi 192 (Breton); Glasgow v 3. 2 (Beneventan). The Visigothic forms are, e.g.: epstła, eptła, epsła (or aepsła), as in Madrid, Bibl. Acad. Hist. 10007 and 25; Manchester, Rylands 83. (Compare the forms for 'apostolus,' above, s.v.)

ergo, igitur. The ancient Notae (eḡ, iḡ) have not been noted at all in this period. The rival (eꝛ̄) of the former appears in the Anglosaxon MS., Frankfort, St Barthol. 32 (Fulda, "saec. ix post."), and in the late Welsh MS., [Cambridge, Corp. Christi 199] (of 1085–1091). In the latter g̊ is the usual form.

The two-letter suspension (ig'), with its suspension-stroke converted into an apostrophe, is not uncommon in Irish and Welsh MSS., such as: the Macdurnan Gospels (Irish); Leyden 88 (with Irish abbreviation); Cambridge, Corp. Christi 153 and [199] (both Welsh); Oxford, Bodl. 572 (Cornish?); and in Lambeth 431 (ff. 145–160), from Llanthony, we find ig² on ff. 146ᵛ and 147ᵛ, a form possibly influenced both by the ancient Nota iḡ and the now common *igit*². But the simpler form (g̓) steadily gains supremacy, particularly in Continental script, e.g. Berne 363 (Irish); [Oxford,

Bodl., Rawl. B 502] (Irish). No instance has been noted of its occurrence in an Anglosaxon MS., and it is only in Continental script that we find it frequently, e.g.: Rome, Vitt. Eman., Sess. 44 and 45; Berne 292; Cologne 53 and 113 and 143; Autun 45; Laon 135; Brit. Mus., Reg. 6 A v.

It is noteworthy that where 'igitur' is ǥ the similar form (g̊) occurs for 'ergo.' The frequency of the latter form shews that the 'igitur' one-letter abbreviation is derived from it. Examples are: (Irish) Berne 363; the Macdurnan Gospels; the Southampton Psalter; [Vienna 1247],

(Welsh) Cambridge Ff IV 32; the [Ricemarch Psalter],

(Cornish?) Oxford, Bodl. 572,

(Continental) Rome, Vitt. Eman., Sess. 44 and 45; Berne 292; Stuttgart H. B. VII 29; Autun 45; St Omer 765; Paris 1761; Cambridge Ee II 4; Cologne 113; Oxford, Bodl. 828; Brit. Mus., Reg. 6 A v; [Leyden 118] (Beneventan); Manchester, Rylands 7.

It appears also in the Anglosaxon Exeter charter 2070 (of 993).

The longer 'igitur' is more often written in full than 'ergo.' It can, of course, be shortened by the use of the Syllable-symbol of 'tur.'

est, (potest), esse. Both forms of abbreviation, the so-called Insular (÷) and the Continental (ē), still represent 'est' in our period. Beneventan script still normally employs the Insular symbol, e.g.: Rome, Vitt. Eman., Sess. 56; Paris 335; Glasgow V 3. 2. The last of these MSS. shews the horizontal stroke replaced by one descending obliquely from left to right. The first two use the Continental symbol (ē) as well. And in [Leyden 118] this latter symbol alone is used.

Turning to Insular script we find:

(Welsh.) Here the Continental form has hardly penetrated; it appears however in Cambridge, Corp. Christi 153. This MS. shows a not uncommon variation of the Insular symbol, replacing either one or both of the dots by commas. Further it writes pot̄ for 'potest' and (on f. 30ʳ) pt̄ for 'possunt.' In the [Ricemarch Psalter], Dublin, Trin. Coll., and [Cambridge, Corp. Christi 199], the 2-form of the Insular symbol is used (with no dot or comma under the horizontal stroke). The Cambridge, Corp. Christi MS. uses pot' for 'potest.'

(Irish.) The Insular symbol (with dots or commas) still easily holds its own, but the Continental appears with it in the Macdurnan Gospels (at least once) and in Cambridge, Corp. Christi 279, though in this latter MS. only the Continental form is found in compounds, 'potest,' 'prodest.' In the [Book of Deer] the compound 'potest' sometimes has the extraordinary forms p^t ÷ and p^o ÷. (Breton.) Breton MSS. seem to admit the Continental symbol freely. Paris 3182 uses it alone. Oxford, Laud. lat. 26 and Cambridge, Corp. Christi 192 and Brit. Mus., Cotton Otho E XIII all use it along with the Insular. (Anglosaxon.) The Continental symbol has still gained no firm footing. It accompanies the Insular in Lambeth 149 (ff. 1–138); Cassel theol. F 25; Cambridge, Corp. Christi 389.

In Continental script both forms are in use in many MSS., some indeed from Insular centres or written by Italian scribes; but others, with no apparent reason for the use of Insular symbols, incline us to the suggestion made in 'Notae Latinae' (p. 73) that the Insular 'est' symbol should rather be called the cursive symbol. Examples are: Paris 1761 (N. Italy); Paris 12296 (Corbie); Berne 128 and 167 and 172 and 236; Trèves, Stadtbibl. 170; Cologne 53 and 113; Autun 15 and 45 (in both only one scribe uses the Insular symbol) and 31; Laon 50 and 97 and 135 and 136 and 428 and 468; St Omer 765; Oxford, Bodl. 828; Brit. Mus., Harley 3017; Cambridge Ee II 4; Brussels 10470–3; Lambeth 325. In Cologne 143 and Autun 22 and 71 and Brit. Mus., Add. 22820 ē is normal, the Insular symbol rare. In St Omer 342 bis the Insular symbol is a common 'signe de renvoi' but occasionally denotes 'est,' though ē is the normal abbreviation.

For all that, ē is the usual form in Continental script. Careful scribes still place it between two dots (though the first one is sometimes omitted).

Spanish script still admits of no abbreviation of 'est' nor of 'esse.' An exception is Manchester, Rylands 89 (of 949 A.D.), where · ē · is frequent (occasionally there are two horizontal strokes over the e).

The abbreviation (ēe) of 'esse' is found in all MSS. of this period, except Spanish (also ēem 'essem,' ēet 'esset,' etc.; even necēe 'necesse'). In e.g. Berne 292, Cologne 53 and 113, instead of the single horizontal abbreviation-stroke, we find a small s-shaped stroke above each e.

et. The 7-form of symbol remains frequent in Insular script. (Examples need not be given.) It is found occasionally in Continental script where it cannot always be traced to Insular influence, e.g.: Berne 207 and 292; Cologne 113; Autun 31 and 45; St Omer 765; Laon 468; Brit. Mus., Harley 3017 (Fleury); Cambridge, Corp. Christi 223. In the following three MSS. the symbol is much smaller and has a projection to the right at the base, the whole resembling an angular *s* or *z*: Berne 128 and 167; Basel B ɪ vi (by one scribe).

etiam. The original Insular symbol (et with abbreviation-stroke transecting the stem of the *t*) survives in Berne 207 (Fleury). The ordinary Irish and Welsh 3-letter symbol (etī) occurs e.g. in: (Irish) the Macdurnan Gospels; [Oxford, Bodl., Rawl. B 502], (Welsh) Cambridge, Corp. Christi 153 and [199]; the [Ricemarch Psalter]; Cambridge Ff ɪv 32, (Cornish?) Oxford, Bodl. 572.

No instances of an abbreviation of 'etiam' in Anglosaxon or Continental script have been noted in this period.

facio. The Insular suspension faē 'factum' has been noted only in the Macdurnan Gospels, along with the contraction fēm 'factum,' fēa 'facta,' fēo 'facto.' (For faē 'facit' see the Syllable-symbol '-it.')

In the early MSS. shewing examples of faē 'factum' (see 'Notae Latinae' p. 79) the contraction had generally occurred also; and the latter seems now to have almost completely ousted the former in both Irish and Welsh. No Anglosaxon examples have been noted, and the forms have not been found in Continental script. We may cite:

(Irish) the Southampton Psalter (fēs 'factus,' fēae 'factae'); [Oxford, Bodl., Rawl. B 502] (fēi, etc.); the [Book of Deer] (fēm), (Cornish?) Oxford, Bodl. 572 (fēa, fēi), (Welsh) [Cambridge, Corp. Christi 199] (fēi); the [Ricemarch Psalter] (fēa, fēm, fēs).

Only one other part of this verb has been found abbreviated, the present infinitive active 'facere,' which in the [Ricemarch Psalter] occurs as fēre.

famulus. The Visigothic symbol (fmls) may be cited from Madrid, Bibl. Nac. 10007 (fmli 'famuli'); Brit. Mus., Add. 25600 (fmĭam 'famulam'); and in a contemporary gloss on f. 106ʳ of Manchester, Rylands 89 (fmĭos).

fīlius. This word (and occasionally 'filia' also) is fairly frequently abbreviated in our period in Irish and Welsh script, e.g.:

(Irish) the Macdurnan Gospels (flŝ, flī, flōs, flīs, flm̄); Berne 363 (flŝ); the Southampton Psalter (flōs); [Oxford, Bodl., Rawl. B 502] (flĭs, flĭi, flĭa),

(Cornish?) Oxford, Bodl. 572 (flōs and flīos),

(Welsh) Cambridge Ff ɪᴠ 32 (flŝ); [Cambridge, Corp. Christi 199] (flŝ, flīi, flm̄, flō and flīo); the [Ricemarch Psalter] (flŝ, flm, flĭi, flŏrum, flĭis, flŏs, flăb;).

flagellum. The Visigothic contraction appears, e.g. in Manchester, Rylands 83 (flīgli 'flagelli').

fortis, etc. The Macdurnan Gospels (fte 'forte') and the [Ricemarch Psalter] (f̄titudo 'fortitudo') use the late Syllable-symbol of 'or' to shorten the word.

frater, mater, pater. The only survival of the ancient Nota (f̄f̄) for 'fratres' that has been noted in this period is Paris 335 (Beneventan); and this MS. uses the common symbol (f̄rs) also.

The contraction (frās), from the three-letter suspension (frā), has been found in the last-mentioned Beneventan MS. and in St Omer 33 bis. Similarly Cologne 53 has frāe 'fratre' and Berne 128 frām (along with frēm) 'fratrem.' The suspension itself appears in Berne 292 (f. 56ʳ frā 'fratres').

The ubiquitous contraction (f̄rs), from the two-letter suspension (f̄r), is of so general use for 'fratres' in every kind of script that we need not give examples. The nominative singular form f̄r 'frater,' while not occurring so often as f̄rs, is still widely used. (Examples are needless, as also of f̄ris 'fratris,' f̄ri 'fratri,' etc.)

A rival suspension for 'frater' (frt̄) is found in: Berne 128; Munich 13038; Laon 468; Orléans 79; Cologne 53 and 143; Autun 31 (along with nr̄t 'noster,' a form that is inexplicable unless we ascribe it to false analogy of f̄rt 'frater'). Of the contraction (frt̄r) from this suspension the only example noted is Berne 128 (frt̄re 'fratre').

The peculiarly Spanish form (f̄rr) may be illustrated from: Madrid, Bibl. Acad. Hist. 24; Madrid, Bibl. Nac. 10007; Manchester, Rylands 104.

The more precise frēs 'fratres' occurs e.g. in:
(Irish) the Macdurnan Gospels; [Oxford, Bodl., Rawl. B 502],
(Welsh) the [Ricemarch Psalter],
(Breton) Brit. Mus., Cotton Otho E xiii,
(Continental) Berne 128 and 236; Düsseldorf B 80.
In 'Notae Latinae' p. 87 f̄rm is called the normal symbol for
'fratrem,' while f̄rum represents 'fratrum.' In our period f̄rm is
coming to be used more and more for the genitive plural, while the
more precise f̄rem is reserved for 'fratrem.' Consequently f̄rum is
dying out as the symbol for the genitive plural (e.g. St Gall 7;
Cambridge, Corp. Christi 192; Lambeth 149 (ff. 1–138); Brit. Mus.,
Add. 11852). But there is still plenty of opportunity for confusion
in the transitional cases where f̄rm denotes in one place 'fratrem,'
in another 'fratrum.' In Brussels 1370, where frēm is used for the
accusative singular, we find f̄rum for the genitive plural, and also
one occurrence of f̄rm corrected by the scribe himself to f̄rem. So
too in Lambeth 431 (ff. 145–160), where the normal forms are
frēm 'fratrem,' frm̄ 'fratrum,' on f. 148ᵛ the scribe corrects f̄rm to
frēm.

To the abbreviation of 'frater' Irish and Welsh scribes add an
analogous abbreviation of 'mater' and 'pater,' mr̄, mr̄is, mr̄i, etc.,
pr̄, pr̄is, pr̄i, etc. (in the Anglosaxon script of Boulogne 90 we find
pr̄, pr̄is, pr̄i, pr̄em, pr̄m 'patrum'; and in the Carolingian Brit. Mus.,
Cotton Titus D xxvii (written at Newminster) pr̄e, pr̄i). Here again
it will be seen that the more precise forms mr̄em, pr̄em are used
for the accusative singular. No instances of the genitive plural
symbol introducing the u have been noted except pr̄um in the
Beneventan script of Glasgow v 3. 2. This MS. too is one of the
rare instances of a non-Insular scribe using these abbreviations,
though we find the unique pt̄r 'pater,' pt̄ri 'patri,' and on f. 43ʳ
pt̄rē 'patrem' ('quod iurabit ad abraham ptrē nsm') in the Visigothic
Manchester, Rylands 89 (of 949).

gens. This word has not been found abbreviated in the singular,
but in Rome, Vitt. Eman., Sess. 44 and 45, two MSS. of Nonantola,
gs̄ stands for 'gentes' (44 f. 3ʳ 'super gentes et super regna'; f. 3ʳ
'fremuerunt gentes'; f. 26ʳ; f. 117ᵛ). Similarly on f. 153ᵛ of Lambeth Palace 431 ("saec. xi," from Llanthony) 'Nolite, inquit, solliciti
esse quid manducetis aut quid bibatis aut quid operamini; haec

enim gŝ inquirunt.' In the Visigothic Manchester, Rylands 89 we find gn̄ts denoting 'gentes.'

Lowe (Loew) 'Beneventan Script' (p. 181) ascribes the gŝ abbreviation to Beneventan script of "saec. xi."

genus. Berne 207 (Fleury) shews gn̄s for 'genus,' among its many capricious symbols for technical grammatical terms. The Welsh MS., Cambridge, Corp. Christi 153, has gn̄s, gn̄is, gn̄e, gn̄m 'generum,' gn̄ales 'generales.' It is a MS. of Martianus Capella. There is certainly a current symbol of the word after our period in the Irish MS. [Oxford, Bodl., Rawl. B 502] in the form gr̄is 'generis,' gr̄e 'genere,' etc.

gloria, gratia. The symbols gła and gr̄a generally co-exist in the same MS., so it is convenient to treat them together. In 'Notae Latinae,' p. 95, it is said that their presence in an eighth- or ninth-century MS. affords fair presumption of Italian or Spanish origin or influence. But in our period they have become universal (though, strangely enough, very few examples of gr̄a have been noted in the Spanish MSS. examined). A few instances must suffice: Cologne 53 (głra, gła, gr̄a) and 113 (gła, gr̄a) and 143 (głram, gła; no instance of gr̄a); Autun 15 (gła, głificent 'glorificent,' gr̄a, gr̄am, gr̄as) and 22 (gła, głae, głam, gr̄am) and 45 (gła, gr̄a); St Omer 168 (gr̄a, gr̄ae, gr̄as; no instance of gła) and 765 (gła; no instance of gr̄a); Berne 128 (gła, gr̄a) and 236 (głosus, gr̄a). Of Insular MSS. we mention: Berne 363 (Irish; gr̄ae, gr̄m 'gratiam'); Boulogne 90 (Anglosaxon; gła, gr̄a); Cambridge, Corp. Christi 307 (Anglosaxon; gła); the Exeter charter 2526 (of 1044; gr̄a); [Cambridge, Corp. Christi 199] (Welsh; gła, głae); the [Ricemarch Psalter] (Welsh; gła).

habeo. The Irish contractions (ht̄ 'habet,' hn̄s 'habens,' hr̄e 'habere,' etc.) are still in common use by Irish, Welsh and Breton scribes. Also in Rome, Vitt. Eman., Sess. 44 (Nonantola). The more precise form hēt appears in the Macdurnan Gospels (hēt 'habet,' hēnt 'habent'; but also hn̄tem 'habentem,' hm̄s 'habemus,' etc.) and in Paris 1761 (Caroline minuscule of N. Italy?; hēt); Berne 236 (hēt).

The word may be shortened by the use of the Syllable-symbol of '-it,' hab̄ 'habet,' e.g.: Basel B ı vi; Berne 87 (Luxeuil); [Leyden 118] (Beneventan); Laon 468.

hic, haec, hoc, hunc. The Insular 'haec' symbol (*h* with a horizontal mark to the right of the shaft; while ħ denoted 'huius'), 'hoc' symbol (*h* with a dot or comma above), 'hunc' symbol (hē) are still found in practically all Irish and Welsh (also Breton) MSS. But in the hands of Continental scribes and in the later Insular MSS. they often take wrong forms. Thus the Anglosaxon Lambeth 149 (ff. 1–138) has 'h' with a horizontal stroke above for 'haec' (and h' for hoc). Basel O IV 17 (Anglosaxon of Fulda) shews for 'haec' the 'hoc' symbol on f. 38ᵛ and the 'autem' h-symbol on f. 34ᵛ. The Irish script of the Macdurnan Gospels and the Welsh script of the [Ricemarch Psalter] and of [Cambridge, Corp. Christi 199] sometimes for 'haec' allow the horizontal stroke to transect the shaft of the *h*. In Berne 207 (Fleury) the 'haec' symbol is used for 'hic,' the 'hunc' symbol for 'huic.'

Later Irish MSS., e.g. the Macdurnan Gospels and [Oxford, Bodl., Rawl. B 502], use *h* with suprascript *i* to denote 'hic.'

The Insular symbols of the pronoun may appear also in Beneventan MSS., and other Continental, e.g.: [Leyden 118] (Beneventan; 'haec,' 'hoc'); Rome, Vitt. Eman., Sess. 44 (Nonantola; 'haec,' 'hoc'); Paris 1761 (N. Italy; 'haec,' 'hoc'); Trèves, Stadtbibl. 122 and 170 ('haec'); Brussels 10470–3 ('haec'); Rome, Vitt. Eman., Sess. 45 (Nonantola; 'hoc').

homo. The two-letter suspension (hō) and its declension hōis 'hominis,' hōi 'homini,' etc., are still widely used in Irish and Welsh (and Breton). Occasionally the *o* is suprascript. Italian scribes too use these forms, e.g.: [Leyden 118] (Beneventan); Rome, Vitt. Eman., Sess. 44 and 45 (Nonantola). Also, e.g.: Munich 13038 (Ratisbon; hō); but they are rare in Continental script. Of Beneventan script Lowe (Loew) 'Beneventan Script' (p.182) says: "My first instances date from the beginning of the 11th century."

Of the intrusion of *i* into these symbols examples are:

(Welsh) Cambridge Ff IV 32 (hōium); the [Ricemarch Psalter] (hōium and hōum),

(Cornish?) Oxford, Bodl. 572 (hōies and hōes),

(Beneventan) [Leyden 118] (hōie, hōium and hōum).

huius (see 'cuius').

idem. No example has been noted of iđ 'idem.' Probably this now ambiguous symbol has retired in favour of iđ 'id est' (see below).

ideo. The form idō still persists in Spain, e.g.: Madrid, Bibl. Nac. 10007; Madrid, Bibl. Acad. Hist. 10067; Manchester, Rylands 104 and 89.

It is known to Italy; witness its occurrence in Rome, Vitt. Eman., Sess. 44 and 45 (Nonantola). Also in Autun 15; Brit. Mus., Harl. 3017 (Fleury); Berne 87 (Luxeuil; with abbreviation-stroke transecting the shaft of the *d*); the Exeter Anglosaxon charter 2521 (of 967); the Anglosaxon Lambeth 149 (ff. 1–138); Lambeth 237 (ff. 146–208, from Llanthony?).

id est. The Insular symbol (i ÷ or I ÷) and the Insular 'cursive' form (·i·) persist in Insular script. The latter appears even in some Continental script, e.g.: Munich 13038 (by one scribe); Berne 167 and 169; St Omer 168. And along with the Continental symbol (id̄) in e.g.: Rome, Vitt. Eman., Sess. 45 (Nonantola); Cologne 53; Berne 128 (sometimes ·ī·). The Beneventan [Leyden 118] also admits the Insular along with the Continental symbol.

In Spain (though the Continental is occasionally admitted, as in Madrid, Bibl. Acad. Hist. 25 and Manchester, Rylands 104) the contractions (id̄t, id̄s, id̄st) are usual, e.g. Manchester, Rylands 83 and 89. It is noteworthy that one scribe of Autun 31 frequently employs id̄t, the Spanish symbol. Also that Munich 6262 (Freising) shews the redundant id̄·ē· beside the normal id̄. Similarly the Breton Brit. Mus., Cotton Otho E XIII shews the redundant ·i·÷.

Iesus (see 'Christus').

igitur (see 'ergo').

in (see the Letter-symbol 'n').

inter. The Insular symbol (I with oblique stroke through it from left up to right) still persists in Irish, Welsh and Anglosaxon script. We have no examples from Continental MSS. except one from the Insular centre Laon (no. 468).

item. The ancient Nota (it̄) seems to survive mainly (but not entirely) in Spain, e.g.: Madrid, Bibl. Nac. 10007; Brit. Mus., Add. 30852. In Insular script it may have been discarded through fear of confusion with the frequent īt 'inter.'

loquitur. The Insular symbol (loq̄r) appears in Berne 363 (Irish). Generally this word is shortened by use of the 'qui' symbol (see below, s.v.).

mater (see 'frater').

meus, suus, (tuus). In Continental (and Beneventan and Visigothic) script the contraction (m̄s) is still commonly used for 'meus.' It seems to be rather less frequent in Insular, e.g.:

(Irish) Berne 363; the Macdurnan Gospels; the Southampton Psalter; the [Book of Deer],

(Welsh) the [Ricemarch Psalter],

(Anglosaxon) Boulogne 90; Basel O iv 17.

The same perhaps may be said of m̄m 'meum,' of which Insular examples are:

(Irish) the Macdurnan Gospels; the Southampton Psalter; [Oxford, Bodl., Rawl. B 502]; the [Book of Deer],

(Welsh) Cambridge, Corp. Christi 153 and [199]; the [Ricemarch Psalter],

(Cornish?) Oxford, Bodl. 572,

(Anglosaxon) Brit. Mus., Cotton Vitell. C viii.

The other cases of this possessive pronoun are more rarely abbreviated, e.g.:

mā 'mea' in Berne 207 (Fleury); Madrid, Bibl. Nac. 10007 (Visigothic),

mī 'mei,' mō 'meo' in the Madrid MS.,

mōs 'meos' in Rome, Vitt. Eman., Sess. 45 (Nonantola).

For 'suus' only the dative, ablative plural has been found abbreviated (s̄s̄ 'suis'); and this abbreviation is no longer confined to Insular script. Examples are:

(late Irish) [Oxford, Bodl., Rawl. B 502]; the [Book of Deer],

(late Welsh) the [Ricemarch Psalter],

(Breton) Oxford, Laud. lat. 26,

(Continental) Rome, Vitt. Eman., Sess. 44 and 45 (Nonantola); Oxford, Bodl. 828.

Of a 'tuus' abbreviation no example has been noted.

mihi, tibi. The ancient Nota for 'mihi' (ṁ) is still common in Irish, Welsh and Breton MSS. It is widely used in Continental script, sometimes (but not always) traceable to Insular influence, e.g.: Cologne 113 and 143; St Omer 168; Berne 172 and 236 and 292; Paris 1761; Trèves, Stadtbibl. 169; Autun 45; Oxford, Bodl. 828; Leyden 21; Brit. Mus., Cotton Titus D xxvii (written at Newminster); Lambeth 204 (from Ely) and 427 (Anglosaxon glosses);

Munich 13038; Rome, Vitt. Eman., Sess. 45 (Nonantola); [Leyden 118] (Beneventan); Manchester, Rylands 7.

The two-letter suspension (mħ) occurs in: two Nonantola MSS., Rome, Vitt. Eman., Sess. 44 and 71; [Leyden 118] (Beneventan); Paris 1761 (N. Italy).

Two of these MSS., Rome, Vitt. Eman., Sess. 44 and [Leyden 118], use also miħ 'mihi.' This three-letter form is found too in Rome, Vitt. Eman., Sess. 45 (Nonantola), and as a suprascript addition by the scribe in the Beneventan Paris 335.

The 'tibi' symbol (t̊) is still frequent in Irish, Welsh and Breton script. In Continental, e.g.: St Omer 765; Cologne 143; Trèves, Stadtbibl. 169; Berne 292; Manchester, Rylands 7; Lambeth 204 and 431 (ff. 145–160).

misericordia. The Veronese symbol (mā) appears to be dying out. It appears in Paris 1761 (mā, mām, mārum).

The three-letter suspension (mīs) has been noted in Boulogne 90 (Anglosaxon; mīsdissimus) and Oxford, Bodl. 572 (Cornish?). The following forms may have been developed from it:

miscđa Paris 12052 (Corbie); Trèves, Dom. 136; Düsseldorf B 80, miscđā St Omer 765; Brussels 1370; Leyden 21; Brit. Mus., Cotton Titus D xxvii,

miscđia Madrid, Bibl. Acad. Hist. 24 (Visigothic); Autun 22; Cambridge Ee ii 4 (and miscđiter); Brit. Mus., Reg. 6 A v; Berne 292; Paris 3182 (Breton), Lambeth 427,

miscđiae and miscđam Autun 15,

misđia Autun 45; the [Ricemarch Psalter] (Welsh),

mīsdia Brit. Mus., Cotton Otho E xiii (Breton).

The Italian symbol (mīa) is still favoured in Italy, but has spread to, e.g.: Cologne 53 and 113 (with micđa, misđia); St Gall 19 (with mcđia, miscđia); Stuttgart H. B. vii 29; [Vienna 1247].

For Visigothic script may be cited:

mrđa, msrcđia, msrđa, mrcđa, mscđa Madrid, Bibl. Nac. 10007, mscđa Madrid, Bibl. Acad. Hist. 24; Brit. Mus., Add. 25600, mscđa and msrēdm Manchester, Rylands 93, mscđa and msđa Manchester, Rylands 104, mscđa, mscđm, miscđa in Manchester, Rylands 89.

Of other capricious abbreviations we may mention: mša [Book of Deer],

miscrdia Exeter charter 2070 (of 993),
misrcdia Autun 17 A,
midia Berne 128.

modo. The ancient Nota (m̊) is still widely used, e.g.:
(Anglosaxon) Boulogne 90; Cassel theol. F 25; Cambridge,
Corp. Christi 389,
(Irish) Berne 363; [Oxford, Bodl., Rawl. B 502],
(Welsh) Cambridge, Corp. Christi 153 and [199]; the [Ricemarch
Psalter],
(Cornish?) Oxford, Bodl. 572,
(Breton) Paris 3182; Cambridge, Corp. Christi 192; Brit. Mus.,
Cotton Otho E xiii,
(Continental) Brussels 1370; Trèves, Dom. 136; Stuttgart H. B.
vii 29; Berne 292; Laon 135; Brit. Mus., Reg. 6 A v; Rome,
Vitt. Eman., Sess. 44 (Nonantola); Lambeth 431 (ff. 145-160).
(Beneventan) [Leyden 118]. Lowe (Loew) 'Beneventan Script'
(p. 185) calls it the standing form from "saec. xi in."

nam. The ancient Nota, *n* with the second upright descending
below the line and traversed by a horizontal stroke, appears in the
Welsh script of Cambridge Ff iv 32 (on f. 43^r) and of Cambridge,
Corp. Christi 153 (on f. 17^r). But in the Cornish (?) script of
Oxford, Bodl. 572 and the Irish of [Oxford, Bodl., Rawl. B 502]
the second upright of a majuscule *N* is extended upwards and
crossed by a horizontal stroke. In Berne 207 (Fleury), on ff. 133^v
and 134^r, *N* is traversed by a vertical stroke hooked towards the left
at the top (easily confusible with the monogram-symbol of 'nisi').

nihil. The monogram-symbol (*N* transected vertically by *L*)
has been noted in Berne 207 (Fleury; also nl).
The two-letter contraction (nl or nl⁻) is confined to Insular
script and not very frequent, e.g.: Berne 363 (Irish); Boulogne 90
(Anglosaxon); Cambridge, Corp. Christi 153 (Welsh); Oxford,
Bodl. 572 (Cornish?); [Oxford, Bodl., Rawl. B 502] (late Irish);
the [Ricemarch Psalter] (late Welsh).

nisi. The monogram-symbol appears in Berne 207 (Fleury) on
f. 30^v, f. 31^r, f. 47^v, etc., *N* traversed vertically by tall minuscule *s*.
The Insular symbol (n̊) is frequent in Irish, Welsh and Breton
MSS. It has also been noted in: Berne 292; Munich 13038
(Ratisbon); [Leyden 118] (Beneventan); Lambeth 204.

nobis, vobis. The two-letter symbols (nƀ, uƀ) are now very rare. The only examples noted are: Berne 363 (Irish; nƀ, uƀ); Frankfort, St Barthol. 32 (Anglosaxon of Fulda; nƀ and noƀ); Brit. Mus., Add. 22820 (Cluny, of 948–994; nƀ). The three-letter symbols (noƀ, uoƀ) are still of universal occurrence, though very little used in Insular, particularly Anglosaxon, script. Insular examples are:
(Irish) the [Book of Deer],
(Welsh) Cambridge, Corp. Christi 153 and [199],
(Breton) Berne 167; Brit. Mus., Cotton Otho E XIII; Cambridge, Corp. Christi 192,
(Cornish?) Oxford, Bodl. 572,
(Anglosaxon) Oxford, Hatton 93.
Visigothic scribes have a habit of using, instead of an abbreviation-stroke, a cedilla under the *b* or the Visigothic 'us' symbol over the *b*.

nomen. The initial-letter suspension (ñ) of 'nomine' has been noted in a MS. from Nonantola, Rome, Vitt. Eman., Sess. 71 (f. 94^v in ñ dñi 'in nomine Domini').
The contractions (nñ 'nomen,' nñe 'nomine') derived from this suspension have been noted in three Visigothic MSS., Brit. Mus., Add. 30852 and 25600 and Madrid, Bibl. Nac. 10007. Brit. Mus., Add. 25600 has also nña 'nomina' and nñatur 'nominatur'; nñe 'nomine' occurs in the Visigothic Manchester, Rylands 89 (a contemporary gloss on f. 254^r).
But the favourite Irish suspension nō 'nomen' and its derivative contractions nōis 'nominis,' nōi 'nomini,' etc., are by far the most frequently used in our period. Though preponderating in Insular script, they are not confined to it. Examples from Continental script are: [Leyden 118] (Beneventan; nōa, nōabat, nōatur); Rome, Vitt. Eman., Sess. 44 and 45 (Nonantola); Berne 236 and 292; Laon 468; Trèves, Stadtbibl. 169; Autun 22; Lambeth 431 (ff. 145–160); Manchester, Rylands 7 (nōe).
The forms with intrusive *i*, nōia 'nomina,' nōium 'nominum,' etc., have been noted in: the Southampton Psalter (Irish); Oxford, Bodl. 572 (Cornish?); Cambridge, Corp. Christi 153 (Welsh); the Exeter charter 2519 (time of Athelstan) and 2071 (of 1018), and Brit. Mus., Cotton Vesp. A VIII. Lowe (Loew) 'Beneventan

Script' (p. 186) cites Monte Cassino 205 ("saec. xi"; nōe 'nomine,' nōa 'nomina') as the earliest Beneventan example of the contraction of 'nomen,' and adds: "The characteristic forms of the more recent MSS. ("saec. xi ex., xii, xiii") are nōie 'nomine,' nōis 'nominis.'" The three-letter suspension noīm 'nomen' may be regarded as a mere shortening by use of the Syllable-symbol 'en,' unless it denotes 'nomine.' Similarly noīma 'nomina' in Berne 236; Brussels 10470-3, etc. The peculiarly Spanish forms, nm̄n, nm̄na, and nm̄e, nm̄i, etc., may be illustrated by: Madrid, Bibl. Acad. Hist. 25 (nm̄n, nm̄ne, nm̄na); Madrid, Bibl. Nac. 10007 (nm̄n, nm̄e, nm̄ne); Manchester, Rylands 83 (nm̄n, nm̄antur), 104 (nm̄n, nm̄i), and 89 (nm̄n, nmña and nmñe); and Brit. Mus., Add. 25600 (nmña, nm̄n, nmñe, nmīs). The forms nñe and nña have been noted above, under nñ 'nomen.'

non. The ancient Nota (ñ) is still universally employed except in Visigothic script. The word may, of course, be shortened by the use of the letter-suspension 'n' and written nō. (In the Irish abbreviation of Leyden 67 D nō sometimes denotes 'non,' sometimes 'nomen.')

noster, vester. The forms nr̄, nr̄i, nr̄o, etc., and the equivalent ur̄, ur̄i, ur̄o, etc., for 'vester' are now so universally used, except in Spain, that no mention will be made of MSS. that use them and no other symbols. In our examples we will speak only of 'noster,' as it is of much more common occurrence than 'vester'; but, as the formation of their symbols is analogous, our remarks may be applied to 'vester' also.

It would appear that scribes still allow themselves much licence in abbreviating these common pronouns. We will consider first the symbols derived from the initial suspension (ñ), ñi 'nostri,' nō 'nostro,' etc. Examples of the combination of these earlier forms with the current nr̄i, nr̄o, etc., are: Rome, Vitt. Eman., Sess. 45 (Nonantola; nm̄ and nr̄m, nr̄a); Berne 207 (Fleury; ñi, ño, and nr̄i, etc.); Basel O IV 17 (Anglosaxon of Fulda; ñi, ñm, and nr̄i, etc.); Munich 13038 (Ratisbon; ñi, ñm, ñis, and nt̄r, nt̄rm, nr̄m); Düsseldorf D 1 (ñm on f. 93ᵛ, and nt̄ sometimes, and ñr, nr̄i, etc., usually).

It is noticeable that in no case are these earlier forms without the *r* used exclusively in any MS.; they appear in Insular, Continental and Beneventan script as mere survivals of an earlier usage. But the statement on p. 152 of 'Notae Latinae' that ñi, etc., "do not survive in MSS. later than about 815" must be qualified in view of our statistics, though the clue for dating there enunciated is not thereby upset. The syllabic suspension (nt̄) is rare in our period. The only example (in addition to Düsseldorf D 1, mentioned above) which has been noted is Épinal 78; and here only one scribe makes use of the form, and he writes nr̄, nr̄i, etc., also. Again there is no exclusive use of the symbol.

An example of the Beneventan ñer 'noster' is Paris 335 (along with ñr). The peculiar form nr̄t (used in company with ñr, nr̄i, etc.) is quite frequently found, e.g.: Basel F v 33; Brussels 10470–3; Trèves, Stadtbibl. 170; Cologne 53 and 143; Autun 22 and 31; Orléans 79; Laon 50 and 135 and 265; St Omer 33 bis; Cambridge, Corp. Christi 272 and 279. The Anglosaxon Boulogne 90 and the Irish Leyden 67 D and the Breton Brit. Mus., Cotton Otho E XIII also shew it. The three-letter form one would expect (nt̄r) occurs (together with nt̄rm 'nostrum') in Munich 13038, as mentioned above. Since the nr̄t form is frequent along with nr̄i, nr̄o, etc., it would seem that it may have arisen from ñr being regarded as a general symbol for all cases of 'noster,' and that the t was added to denote the nominative singular (in preference to another r, which would have conveyed the idea of a plural), just as the other cases were made explicit by the addition of m, o, a, etc. But there is no evidence that ñr ever denoted any other case than the nominative. It is perhaps worth mention that St Omer 765 shews the analogous formation prb̄rt for 'presbyter,' though nr̄t has not been noted in this MS.; also Rome, Vitt. Eman., Sess. 71 has pb̄rt along with the ñr, nr̄i forms.

Perhaps one reason for the multitude of symbols still in use is that, with all their variety, they are not liable to be misunderstood. And the frequent occurrence of the pronoun (in phrases like 'Dominus noster') made scribes seek relief from monotony.

It remains to mention the practice among Spanish scribes. The peculiarly Spanish symbol (ns̄r) still survives, but it is noticeable that the ñr, nr̄i forms also occur in Visigothic script of our period, e.g.: Madrid, Bibl. Acad. Hist. 24 (nsi, nsae, nr̄m); Madrid, Bibl. Nac. 10007 (nsr, nsi, nr̄i, nr̄m); Manchester, Rylands 104 (nsr, nsi, nr̄i), but 83 (nsr, nsi, etc.); Brit. Mus., Add. 30852 (nsr, nsi, nsam, n̄r, nr̄a, nr̄e).

numerus. Welsh and Irish scribes continue to use the forms nūs, nūi, nūo, nūm, etc. Also e.g.: Cambridge, Corp. Christi 192 (Breton); Oxford, Bodl. 572 (Cornish?); Rome, Vitt. Eman., Sess. 44 and 45 (Nonantola). The Irish Berne 363 courts confusion by its similar abbreviation of 'numen' (nūe 'numine,' nūa 'numina') after the analogy of 'nomen.'

nunc, tunc. The older forms (n̊, t̊) still survive occasionally, e.g.: Munich 13038; Cologne 143; Berne 207 (Fleury); Paris 1761 (N. Italy); Berne 236; Paris 12052 and 12296 (Corbie; also tc̄).

But nc̄ and tc̄ (generally appearing together) are very frequent in Insular script, and also in Continental (by Insular influence?). Continental examples are e.g.: Brit. Mus., Reg. 6 A v; Brit. Mus., Cotton Vesp. B vi; Berne 128; Munich 6262 (nc̄ and t̊); Trèves, Stadtbibl. 169 and 122 and 170; Stuttgart H. B. vii 29; Cologne 53; Autun 45; Laon 50; St Omer 765; Rome, Vitt. Eman., Sess. 45. Only nc̄ has been noted in: Rome, Vitt. Eman., Sess. 44; St Gall 7; Lambeth 204 and 431 (ff. 145–160); Autun 15; Laon 468; Épinal 78; [Leyden 118] (Beneventan). Only tc̄ in: Cologne 13; Berne 292.

omnino (see 'omnis').

omnipotens. It seems needless to discuss the capricious abbreviation of this frequently abbreviated word. The commonest forms are omp̄s 'omnipotens,' omp̄is 'omnipotentis,' etc., but we find also omn̄ps, omnip̄s, omp̄tis, omp̄otem, etc.

omnis. The syllabic suspension (om̄) is now almost extinct. The only examples that have been noted are: Brit. Mus., Add. 11852 (f. 46ᵛ 'et omnes stare oportet'); Berne 169 (f. 5ʳ 'omnes'; also om̄s); Épinal 78 (on second last page 'omnes gentes').

The contractions (om̄s 'omnes,' om̄a 'omnia') are so universal in Continental, Beneventan and Visigothic script that examples are needless. Examples from Insular are:

(Anglosaxon) Cambridge, Corp. Christi 307; Boulogne 90; Lambeth 149 (ff. 1–138),

(Irish) the Southampton Psalter; Leyden 67 D,

(Welsh) Cambridge Ff IV 32; Cambridge, Corp. Christi 153; the [Ricemarch Psalter].

The use of om̄s for 'omnis,' as well as for 'omnes,' is now rare and in many instances a corrector has altered to om̄is. Examples are: (Continental) Basel B IV 12 (f. 34ʳ, f. 82ᵛ, f. 125ʳ) and I 6; St Gall 7, Trèves, Stadtbibl. 170; Cologne 53 (f. 71ʳ); St Omer 33 bis (f. 18ᵛ) and 342 bis (f. 96ʳ); Paris 3182 (Breton), (Welsh) Cambridge, Corp. Christi 153 (f. 7ʳ, f. 47ᵛ). All the above use om̄s freely to denote 'omnes' also.

The usual form for 'omnis' is om̄is. Continental examples are needless, also Visigothic and Beneventan. Insular are rare, e.g.: Boulogne 90 (Anglosaxon); Lambeth 149 (ff. 1–138, Anglosaxon); Leyden 67 D (Irish); Oxford, Bodl. 572 (Cornish?).

A variant (om̄ia) of om̄a 'omnia' is of fairly frequent occurrence (generally along with om̄a), though no example has been noted from Insular script. And while om̄m 'omnium' (Munich 6262, on f. 26ᵛ, f. 79ᵛ) or 'omnem' (Munich 13038) is unusual, om̄ium and om̄em are the current forms.

By the use of the letter-symbol for m the word may be shortened, e.g.: ōne 'omne' in Paris 12296 and ōnem 'omnem' in Laon 136; ōnibus 'omnibus' in Épinal 78. And the form om̄ñs 'omnes' (e.g. Munich 13038; Laon 265; St Omer 765; Paris 335) might be called a use of the letter-symbol of e as fairly as a contraction from the three-letter suspension.

It remains to consider the peculiarly Insular symbols (ōis, ōe, ōi, ōes, ōia, ōium, ōibus). In our period the distinction between Irish (with Welsh) and Anglosaxon seems still to hold. No instances of these forms have been noted in Anglosaxon MSS.; only the Continental forms, e.g.: Cambridge, Corp. Christi 389 (ōmi) and 307 (om̄s, om̄a); Boulogne 90 (om̄is, om̄s, om̄a). The Cornish (?) Oxford, Bodl. 572 shews the two varieties (ōis, ōi, ōia, ōibus and om̄is, om̄s, om̄a, om̄ia, om̄um, om̄ibus). So does the Beneventan [Leyden 118] (ōis, ōi, ōe, ōem, ōs 'omnes,' ōia, ōium, ōibus, ōino 'omnino,' and om̄em, om̄i, om̄s, om̄ia, om̄a, om̄ium, om̄ibus). For the rest, Welsh and Irish scribes occasionally introduce the very common forms om̄s and om̄a along with the Insular, e.g.: Cambridge Ff IV 32 (Welsh; om̄s, om̄a, ōa, ōe); Cambridge, Corp. Christi 153 (Welsh;

ōis, ōe, ōes, ōa, om̄i, om̄s) and [199] (Welsh; ōis, ōe, ōium, ōia, ōibus, ōino 'omnino,' om̄s); the [Ricemarch Psalter] (Welsh; ōes rarely, om̄s usually, ōis, ōi, etc.). Of Beneventan Lowe (Loew) 'Beneventan Script' (p. 187) says: "The second system, which dates from the 11th century, is typical of the recent MSS. and has forms like oīs, oēm, ōi, ōe, ōs 'omnes,' oīa or ōa, om̄m and oibus."

pater (see 'frater').

per, prae, pro. In all Continental script (except Visigothic) the universal symbol of 'per' is *p* with an horizontal stroke through the shaft, whether 'per' be the preposition or a mere syllable (initial, medial, final). Visigothic continues to use the Continental 'pro' symbol (*p* with curve prolonged through the shaft) to denote 'per' and writes 'pro' in full. But the Visigothic MS., Brit. Mus., Add. 30852, shews beside the normal Visigothic symbol the Continental symbol (sometimes with a hook on the left of the horizontal stroke).

The peculiarly Insular symbol (*p* with a 'tail') is the only form used in some MSS., e.g.: Brit. Mus., Cotton Vitell. C VIII (Anglosaxon); Berne 207 (Fleury). But the Continental symbol appears along with it in such MSS. as: Oxford, Bodl. 572 (Cornish?); Boulogne 90 (Anglosaxon); Cassel theol. F 25 (Anglosaxon of Fulda); Basel O IV 17 (Anglosaxon of Fulda; the Continental symbol in the first half, the Insular in the second); the Macdurnan Gospels (Irish); [Oxford, Bodl., Rawl. B 502] (late Irish); the [Book of Deer] (late Irish); Leyden 67 D (also p' a form like the 'pri' and 'post' symbols); Cambridge Ff IV 32 (Welsh); Cambridge, Corp. Christi 153 (Welsh). In the other Anglosaxon MSS. of this period that have been examined only the Continental symbol has been found, e.g.: Lambeth 218; Cambridge, Corp. Christi 307 and 389. Also the Southampton Psalter (Irish) and [Cambridge, Corp. Christi 199] (late Welsh) shew the Continental symbol only.

Of 'prae' (or 'pre') the symbol (p̄) is used in all scripts (except Visigothic, which still refuses to abbreviate this syllable), although there is still evidence of a preference for writing it in full, e.g.: always in Paris 335 (Beneventan); Oxford, Bodl. 828; Brit. Mus., Harl. 3017; St Gall 19 and 46; Munich 13038; St Omer 342 bis. And in our period precision is given to the symbol in various ways. Thus it gets a cedilla (expressive of 'ae') appended to it on f. 34ᵛ

of Laon 136. In Berne 363 (Irish) p with two commas above it
(the symbol of 'pra') accompanies the normal form. In Berne 128
p with open a above it (another symbol of 'pra') plays the same
part; also in Autun 31. But in this last MS. the commoner form
of our period (p̄ with open a above) is also used. (We may compare
p̄ with o above for the first syllable of 'proelium' in Autun 45.) This
commoner form is the sole symbol of 'prae' in Stuttgart H. B. VII 29
(of 1034–1046) and accompanies p̄ in such MSS. as: Munich 6262
(Freising, of 854–875); Düsseldorf D 1 (Essen, of 868–872);
Cambridge Ee II 4 ("saec. x in."); Brussels 10470–3 ("saec. x");
Paris 12052 (Corbie, of 945–986); Brit. Mus., Add. 22820 (Cluny,
of 948–994); St Omer 168 and 765 (St Bertin, of 987–1007);
Lambeth 204 ("saec. x–xi"). Generally the suprascript a is of the
open form, but the round form also occurs in Düsseldorf D 1.
We may therefore find in p̄ with suprascript a 'prae' a clue to
dating.

There are no developments in the use of the 'pro' symbol during
our period. Visigothic scribes continue to write the syllable in full.
On f. 358^r of the Visigothic Manchester, Rylands 89 the corrector
(probably the scribe himself) has crossed out the wavy tail of the
p and substituted a suprascript o in order to change the sense
from 'per' to 'pro.'

populus. A variety of symbols are still found. The characteristic
Insular form (pl̄s, pl̄i, etc.) is still used in Insular MSS., and sometimes appears in others, e.g.: Munich 6262 (along with ppl̄s, etc.);
Berne 128 (occasionally); Rome, Vitt. Eman., Sess. 44 (Nonantola;
usually corrected to ppl̄s); [Leyden 118] (Beneventan).

The characteristic Visigothic form (ppl̄s, ppl̄i, etc.) is still used
in Spanish MSS. and indeed in all Continental script, e.g.: Paris 335
(Beneventan); Paris 3182 (Breton); Brit. Mus., Cotton Otho E XIII
(Breton); Brit. Mus., Add. 22820 (Cluny); St Gall 46; Munich
6262 (also ppl̄us, ppl̄um); Munich 13038; Berne 128; Laon 428;
Cologne 113; Rome, Vitt. Eman., Sess. 44 and 45 and 71
(Nonantola); Manchester, Rylands 7 (Prüm).

The more explicit form (popl̄s, popl̄i, etc.) is fairly common too
in all Continental script, e.g.: Paris 3182 (Breton); Berne 87 and
292; Brit. Mus., Add. 24142; Cologne 53 and 113 and 143; Autun
15 and 22 and 45; Trèves, Stadtbibl. 169 and 170; Frankfort, St

Barthol. 32 (Anglosaxon of Fulda); Rome, Vitt. Eman., Sess. 45 (Nonantola).

The three-letter suspension (poṗ) and its derivative contraction (poṗs, poṗi, etc.) have not been found in this period.

The two-letter suspension (p̄p̄) persists rarely, e.g.: Leyden 67 D (under Irish influence); [Leyden 118] (Beneventan). In Berne 207 (Fleury; also p̄p̄is 'populis') it shews suprascript *s*, *m*, *o* and no abbreviation-stroke. To Beneventan Lowe (Loew) 'Beneventan Script' (p. 188) ascribes the forms pꝑ 'populi,' pꝓ 'populo' from "saec. xi in."

Variants are p̄p̄s of the Breton Paris 3182 and ppł 'populus' of Cambridge, Corp. Christi 279; also ppułis 'populis' of the Visigothic Madrid, Bibl. Acad. Hist. 10007. In Berne 363 (Irish) we find płatur 'populatur.'

post. In Insular script the characteristic symbols (pᵗ and pᵒ) continue in common use, the former appearing even in the Continental script of Düsseldorf D 1 (Essen; occasionally), the latter in Cambridge Ee ii 4 and Autun 31 and Oxford, Bodl. 828 (along with p'), and Brit. Mus., Cotton Titus D xxvii (written at Newminster).

An alternative type of the former (p̄t) is found in e.g.: Cassel theol. F 25 (Anglosaxon of Fulda); Laon 265 (with a comma over the *t* instead of the abbreviation-stroke); Laon 50 (occasionally expanded by suprascript 'os'); Rome, Vitt. Eman., Sess. 44, f. 2ʳ (Nonantola; with abbreviation-stroke over both the *p* and the *t*, thus rendering the word liable to confusion with 'praeter').

Thus the Insular symbols are still largely employed in their own script and have penetrated very little into Continental.

The Continental symbol (p') persists throughout the Continent (not Spain) and even appears in the Anglosaxon Lambeth 149 (ff. 1–138); Cambridge, Corp. Christi 279 (in the Irish marginal glosses), etc. The apostrophe is the 'us' symbol; and in Berne 207 (Fleury) another 'us' symbol is used (p;). Some scribes, e.g. Berne 128, use p' 'pos' (e.g. p'tremo 'postremo,' ap'toli 'apostoli').

Visigothic script does not abbreviate 'post' at all.

potest. The three-letter ancient Nota (pot̄) occurs in Cambridge, Corp. Christi 153 and [199] (both Welsh): the latter replaces the abbreviation-stroke over the *t* by a comma.

The form p̄t occurs in the former, and (with the *t* suprascript and the Insular 'est' symbol added) in the [Book of Deer] (also *p* with suprascript *o* before the Insular 'est' symbol). The usual method of shortening the word is by employment of an 'est' symbol (pot ÷, potē, etc.).

prae (see 'per').

praeter. The common p̄t is really a combination of the 'prae' and 'ter' symbols.

pro (see 'per').

proprius. The so-called monogram symbol (of 'pro' and 'pri') still remains in Irish and Welsh script, e.g.: Leyden 67 D (Irish); Cambridge, Corp. Christi 153 (Welsh); Oxford, Bodl. 572 (Cornish?). But more common is the practice of writing the 'pro' and 'pri' symbols side by side to represent 'propri' and adding the termination, e.g.: the Macdurnan Gospels (Irish); the [Ricemarch Psalter] (Welsh); Autun 15 and 45; Laon 464; Berne 128; Rome, Vitt. Eman., Sess. 45 (Nonantola).

propter. The ancient Nota (p̄p̄) and the alternative form (pp with abbreviation-stroke traversing the two shafts) continue in use. The former, e.g. in:

(Irish) Leyden 67 D (also denoting 'populum'!); the Macdurnan Gospels; the Southampton Psalter; Berne 363,

(Welsh) Cambridge, Corp. Christi 153; the [Ricemarch Psalter],

(Anglosaxon) the Lambeth Aldhelm; Cassel theol. F 25 (Fulda),

(Breton) Cambridge, Corp. Christi 192; Paris 3182,

(Visigothic) Brit. Mus., Add. 30852,

(Continental) Épinal 78; St Gall 7; Berne 207; Munich 13038; Laon 50; Lambeth 431 (ff. 145–160).

The latter, e.g. in:

(Breton) Cambridge, Corp. Christi 192; Paris 3182; Brit. Mus., Cotton Otho E XIII; Oxford, Laud. lat. 26,

(Anglosaxon) Cambridge, Corp. Christi 389; Boulogne 90; Lambeth 149 (ff. 1–138; also p̄p̄),

(Irish) [Book of Deer],

(Welsh) Cambridge, Corp. Christi 153 and [199],

(Cornish?) Oxford, Bodl. 572,

(Continental) Berne 128.

More precise forms of the two above symbols add to them the
'ter' symbol (ŧ). Of the former, e.g.: Brit. Mus., Add. 24142; Laon
468; Paris 1761 (N. Italy). Of the latter, e.g.: Laon 468; Munich
6262; Brit. Mus., Cotton Otho E XIII. One abbreviation-stroke
sometimes suffices (p͞pt), e.g.: Leyden 67 D; Basel B I vi; Épinal
78; Valenciennes 195 (Anglosaxon); Trèves, Stadtbibl. 170.
The ancient Nota consisting of the 'pro' symbol followed by the
'ter' symbol (and therefore really denoting 'proter' rather than
'propter') occurs in: Oxford, Bodl. 572 (Cornish?); Cologne 53 and
113; Laon 468, etc. Berne 128 uses the 'pro' symbol followed by
the letters 'ter.'
The normal Visigothic modification of the p͞p form (p͞ptr) occurs
e.g. in: Manchester, Rylands 83 and 104 (correctors use also p͞pter,
p͞r, p͞pr). And (along with p͞pr) e.g. in: Madrid, Bibl. Nac. 42 and
10007; Madrid, Bibl. Acad. Hist. 10067. The form p͞pr occurs also
in Madrid, Bibl. Acad. Hist. 25, Manchester, Rylands 89 and Brit.
Mus., Add. 25600 (p͞ptr also).
The Beneventan Paris 335 uses a four-letter suspension (pro͞p).
The monogram form (the normal 'pro' symbol with a tail
attached to the p as in the Insular symbol of 'per') has only been
noticed in one MS. of our period, Cambridge Ff IV 32
(Welsh).
Everywhere the 'pro' or the 'ter' symbol, or both of them, may
be employed to shorten the word.
qua, quo. The ancient Notae (q̊, q̊) are still frequent in Insular
script. They are common too in Breton MSS., e.g.: Cambridge,
Corp. Christi 192; Brit. Mus., Cotton Otho E XIII; Berne 167;
Paris 3182. Continental script admits them, though many of the
following examples are from Insular foundations: Berne 128 and
292; St Omer 33bis and 168 and 765; Laon 428 and 468; Paris
12052 and 12296 (both Corbie); Trèves, Stadtbibl. 170; Munich
13038; Stuttgart H. B. VII 29; Autun 15 and 22 and 45; Cambridge
Ee II 4; Brit. Mus., Harl. 3017 and Add. 22820 and Reg. 6 A v and
Cotton Vesp. A VIII; Rome, Vitt. Eman., Sess. 44 and 45 (Nonantola); Paris 1761 (N. Italy); Manchester, Rylands 98. They are
found in the late Beneventan [Leyden 118], etc.
No examples have been found in Spanish MSS.
quae. The ancient Nota (q̄) is now used in all scripts, Continental

and Insular, but the 'quae' symbol is rare in comparison with those for 'qui' and 'quod.' Insular examples are:

(Irish) Berne 363; the Macdurnan Gospels; the Southampton Psalter; Cambridge, Corp. Christi 279 (with Irish glosses); [Oxford, Bodl., Rawl. B 502]; the [Book of Deer], (Welsh) Cambridge, Corp. Christi 153 and [199], (Cornish?) Oxford, Bodl. 572, (Anglosaxon) Brit. Mus., Cotton Vitell. C VIII.

But there are now many deviations from the strict use of this symbol. In the Anglosaxon Boulogne 90 it denotes 'quam' and 'quem' as well as 'quae.' In the Welsh Cambridge Ff IV 32, the [Ricemarch Psalter], etc., it is made more explicit by the addition under the *q* of the ligature 'æ.' And this explicit form is the sole symbol in [Leyden 118] (Beneventan), Cambridge, Corp. Christi 223, Manchester, Rylands 7, etc., and accompanies other forms in Rome, Vitt. Eman., Sess. 44 (Nonantola), Brit. Mus., Cotton Vesp. B VI (ff. 1–103), etc. A suprascript *a* is added to the normal symbol in Stuttgart H. B. VII 29, etc. And so on. In fact a modification of the normal symbol may be used as a clue to dating.

The Insular symbol (q : ·), often with commas for dots, is still fairly common in Insular script. For example, it is the sole symbol in Cassel theol. F 25 (Anglosaxon of Fulda), and accompanies the Continental symbol in Leyden 67 D (under Irish influence) and Basel O IV 17 (Anglosaxon of Fulda); Brit. Mus., Cotton Otho E XIII (Breton); Berne 207 (Fleury) and 167.

It too is liable to modification in our period, for an abbreviation-stroke is often added.

Other degenerate forms are *q* with abbreviation-stroke through the shaft (really the 'qui' symbol) followed by one dot or two dots (q. and q: properly denote 'que'), e.g. Laon 265; Lambeth 325.

And the 'que' symbol is often used in its various forms. The Visigothic *q* with suprascript small *s* really denotes 'que' but is freely used for 'quae' by Spanish scribes.

quaeritur. The Irish contraction (q̄r) appears in Berne 363 (Irish; also q̄rt 'quaerunt'), Cambridge Ff IV 32 (Welsh), etc.

quaesumus. The liturgical symbol (qs̄) is still common in Continental and Insular MSS., e.g.:

(Insular) Boulogne 90; Frankfort, St Barthol. 32; Oxford, Bodl. 572,

(Continental) Brussels 10470–3; Düsseldorf D 1; Paris 12052 (Corbie); St Omer 342 bis; Cambridge, Corp. Christi 272; Brit. Mus., Cotton Titus D xxvii.

quam. The Insular symbol (*q* with oblique stroke through the shaft, this stroke being hooked at both ends or written quickly as a wavy stroke) is still common in Insular and Breton MSS. It is fairly frequent too in Continental, e.g.:

(the hooked form) Munich 6262 (also qā); Cambridge Ee ii 4; Autun 15; Épinal 78; St Omer 765; Trèves, Stadtbibl. 170; Cologne 113; Berne 207 (Fleury); Manchester, Rylands 98, (the wavy variety) Brussels 1370; Berne 167 (also for 'quod'); Paris 1761.

A short horizontal stroke (as in the 'quia' symbol) is found in Stuttgart H. B. vii 29; Paris 3182 (Breton; also for 'quia'), etc.

The unusual form qā appears in Laon 50 ('numquam' f. 54ʳ); Munich 6262, etc.

The suspension tamq 'tamquam' appears in Brit. Mus., Add. 30852 (Visigothic), etc. And the word may of course be shortened by the use of the 'qua' symbol (q̊m). Brit. Mus., Cotton Vesp. B vi writes *q* with an oblique stroke through the shaft and a suprascript *a* as well as qm̄ to denote 'quam.' A variety of the latter form, with two reversed commas above the *q* instead of the abbreviation-stroke, occurs in Brit. Mus., Cotton Vesp. A viii.

quando. The Irish symbols (qn̄, qño) are common in Irish and Welsh MSS. and both appear (along with qndo) in the Anglosaxon Boulogne 90. Other examples are, e.g.: Autun 15 (qño); Cambridge Ee ii 4 (qño); Paris 12296 (Corbie); Laon 468 (qñ by second scribe). The English form (qn̄d, qnd) occurs e.g. in: Frankfort, St Barthol. 32 (Anglosaxon of Fulda); Berne 167 and 207 (Fleury); Paris 1761 (N. Italy, in 'aliquando'); Paris 3182 (Breton; also qndo); the Anglosaxon Lambeth 149 (ff. 1–138; often corrected to qndo).

The uncommon qdo appears in Oxford, Laud. lat. 26 (Brittany). But fairly common is qndo or qndo, e.g.: Cambridge, Corp. Christi 279; Laon 97; Brit. Mus., Cotton Otho E xiii (Breton); Rome, Vitt. Eman., Sess. 45 (Nonantola).

Of course the word may be shortened by use of the 'qua' symbol.

3-2

quantus. The two forms of abbreviation (qñtm or qñm 'quantum') still persist in Insular script, e.g. qñm, in Cambridge Ff IV 32 (Welsh); Cambridge, Corp. Christi 153 and [199] (Welsh); Oxford, Bodl. 572 (Cornish?; qñm, qña, qño; also qñta, qñto). In all these, as one would expect, 'quoniam' is expressed by qm̄ to avoid confusion. The fuller qñtm occurs e.g. in: Brit. Mus., Cotton Otho E XIII (Breton); Paris 3182 (Breton; qñtum); Boulogne 90 (Anglosaxon; qñta). The last MS. uses qñm, qm̄, quō for 'quoniam.' Shortening by use of the 'qua' symbol is of course found, e.g.: Paris 3182; Berne 128; Rome, Vitt. Eman., Sess. 44.

quare. The ancient Nota (qr̄) may have been used in Berne 207 (also qr̄e), but has been corrected to q̊r̄. The contraction qr̄e appears also e.g. in: the Macdurnan Gospels; Laon 468, etc. The 'qua' symbol may be used to shorten the word.

quasi. The ancient Nota (qs̄) is practically extinct in our period: the only example noted is in Leyden 67 D (under Irish influence). The derivative contraction (qs̄i) is frequent in Insular MSS. (and Breton); also, e.g.: Trèves, Stadtbibl. 122; Munich 6262; Berne 172 (marginalia). Often the 'qua' symbol is employed (q̊si).

que. The various forms of the suspension (q· q' q: q; q;) still persist in all types of MSS., the single-dotted form being perhaps less common now than the others. To give examples is needless. The Visigothic symbol (qˢ) is still in vogue in Spanish MSS. and even appears (along with the usual q:) in Berne 207 (Fleury). When scribes write loq̄ndum, freq̄nter, etc., they misuse the 'quae' symbol to express 'que.' This misuse is very common. The Continental symbol (q with a stroke passing obliquely through the shaft down from right to left) still persists, often in modified form. While the stroke is straight in Berne 128 and 236, etc., it is sinuous in: Laon 97 and 135 and 136, etc. Often the Continental symbol has a dot (or semicolon or the like) added to it, the two 'que' symbols being thus combined into one.

quem. This word is not very often abbreviated in our period, but Irish and Welsh scribes observe carefully their characteristic symbol (q with an abbreviation-stroke above it which is hooked at both ends). The Anglosaxon Boulogne 90 also uses this symbol, but makes it do duty for 'quae' and (occasionally) 'quam' as well.

Épinal 78 uses q̄ (expanded to 'quem' by a corrector). Visigothic scribes add *m* to their 'que' symbol (qᵃm).

The ancient Nota (qm̄) occurs on f. 11ᵛ of Autun 31 in 'quemque,' but no other instance of this symbol has been noted. Probably it gave way before the common use of qm̄ to denote 'quoniam.'

qui. The normal Nota (q́) seems to maintain its claim to the title of the 'Insular' symbol. But Continental examples still occur, some through Insular influence, e.g.: Paris 12052 and 12296 (Corbie); St Omer 33 bis and 168 and 342 bis and 765; Laon 428 and 468; Cologne 143; St Gall 7; Brit. Mus., Cotton Titus D xxvii; Trèves, Stadtbibl. 169 and 170; Munich 6262; Stuttgart H.B. vii 29; Berne 236; Cambridge Ee ii 4; Cambridge, Corp. Christi 223; Brit. Mus., Add. 11852 and 22820 and 24142; Brit. Mus., Harl. 3017; Brit. Mus., Reg. 6 A v; Manchester, Rylands 7 and 98.

This so-called Insular form is definitely more common now (except in Beneventan) than the alternative symbol (*q* with cross-stroke through the shaft). The cross-stroke has three possible forms: (1) horizontal, (2) oblique and hooked at each end (rare), (3) sinuous. In the second and third there might still be confusion with the 'quam' and 'quod' symbols respectively.

The first of the three is still the Beneventan symbol and in general the Italian, e.g. Rome, Vitt. Eman., Sess. 44 and 45 (Nonantola). But it occurs elsewhere too on the Continent, e.g. in: Brussels 10470–3; Laon 50 and 265; Cambridge, Corp. Christi 272; Basel O iv 17 (Anglosaxon of Fulda). It is used along with q́ in such MSS. as: Cologne 53 and 113; Leyden 67 D (under Irish influence); Autun 45; Berne 128, etc. And along with the second of the three also in Laon 136. In the Irish Berne 363 (written in Italy) it has a suprascript *i*. An example of the second (rare) form is Brit. Mus., Cotton Tib. A ii (written in Germany).

The third of the three is almost confined to Visigothic script, where 'quod' is written in full, e.g.: Manchester, Rylands 83; Brit. Mus., Add. 30852; Madrid, Bibl. Acad. Hist. 10067; Madrid, Bibl. Nac. 10007.

In two Visigothic MSS. (both from Cardeña) which admit *q* with sinuous stroke through the shaft for 'quod,' Manchester, Rylands 89 and Brit. Mus., Add. 25600, the rare second form (with oblique cross-stroke hooked at each end) occurs for 'qui,' '-qui-' and 'qui-.'

The scribe of the Anglosaxon Cassel theol. F 25 writes q̄ for 'qui' on f. 48ᵛ (and probably elsewhere, though effaced by the corrector's q̇). This MS. uses q:· for 'quae.'

quia. The Insular symbol (*q* with cross-stroke through its shaft, either horizontal, oblique, or slightly sinuous) remains almost strictly confined to Insular MSS. or to MSS. under Insular influence. Other examples are: Oxford, Bodl. 828 (Exeter); Trèves, Stadtbibl. 122; Berne 167 (with Breton glosses) and 207 (Fleury). It is found along with the Continental symbol in e.g.: Boulogne 90 (Anglosaxon); Paris 3182 (Breton); Brit. Mus., Cotton Otho E xiii (Breton) Munich 6262 (Freising); Basel F v 33 (Fulda).

The Continental symbol (*q* with either a V-shaped mark lying with its point against it, or with a 2-shaped mark) persists in Continental script but has found no foothold in Insular. Stuttgart H. B. vii 29 sometimes adds a suprascript *i* to *q* with 2-mark.

Of course the word is frequently shortened by use of a 'qui' symbol. Brit. Mus., Cotton Vesp. B vi has the peculiar form *q* with a cross-stroke through the shaft and suprascript *ia* at least twice (ff. 3ʳ, 32ʳ).

quibus. This word may be shortened by use of a 'qui' symbol or an '-us' Syllable-symbol or of both. A trace of the ancient Nota (qɓ) appears in the Breton MS., Brit. Mus., Cotton Otho E xiii, in which the forms q̄b: and qɓ occur.

quid. There is still no true symbol of 'quid.' The use of a 'qui' symbol to shorten the word is frequent. Confusion with the 'quod' symbol (qđ) is not very common. Brit. Mus., Cotton Titus D xxvii (written at Newminster) has aliqđ 'aliquid' on f. 28ᵛ and qđ 'quod' on f. 68ʳ, though *q* with sinuous stroke through the shaft is usual for the latter. St Omer 168 shews on f. 49ᵛ and 123ᵛ numqđ and quicqđ and elsewhere uses qđ for 'quod.' This MS. writes also q̇đ for 'quid,' a redundant form that is fairly common, e.g.: Autun 31 and 45; Cologne 53 and 113; Trèves, Dom. 136. The danger of this redundant form is that it is identical with the word 'quidem' (written with the Syllable-symbol of 'em'). The two Cologne MSS. just named use also a now common form qiđ (which may be merely the employment of an abbreviation-stroke to denote suprascript *u*), e.g.: Leyden 88; Laon 135; Trèves, Dom. 136; Trèves, Stadtbibl. 169; Brit. Mus., Add. 22820; Manchester, Rylands 7. In Basel

B I vi, which has qđ 'quod' and seems not to abbreviate 'qui,' the probably arbitrary suspensions aliq 'aliquid,' inq 'inquid,' nūq 'numquid,' etc., occur with cross-stroke through the shaft of *q*.

quippe. The ancient syllabic suspension (qp̄) has been noted in Laon 50 (also quip̄). Scribes often shorten the word by use of a 'qui' symbol.

quis. The usual method of writing 'quis' is to add *s* to either of the 'qui' symbols. The Corbie MS., Paris 12296, shews however the old symbol (qs̄) in the word 'quisquis.' Similarly Rome, Vitt, Eman., Sess. 44 (Nonantola) has, on f. 24ᵛ, qˢqˢ 'quisquis.'

quo (see 'qua').

quod. The Insular symbol (*q* with shaft traversed by a cross-stroke which is normally sinuous) is practically always associated with Insular scribes. Such MSS. as admit it often use also the Continental symbol (qđ), e.g.: Leyden 67 D (under Irish influence) and 88; Berne 167; Rome, Vitt. Eman., Sess. 44 (Nonantola); [Leyden 118] (Beneventan; the Insulár symbol is deformed to *q* with oblique cross-stroke); also the Anglosaxon MSS., Cassel theol. F 25 and Frankfort, St Barthol. 32 and Basel O IV 17; the Welsh, Cambridge, Corp. Christi 153; the Cornish (?) Oxford, Bodl. 572; the Breton, Paris 3182 and Brit. Mus., Cotton Otho E XIII and Cambridge, Corp. Christi 192 (sometimes q' for the Insular symbol) and Berne 207 (Fleury).

The Continental symbol (qđ) is very common. Varieties are:

quđ (e.g.: St Omer 765; Laon 50; Basel B IV 12; Brit. Mus., Add. 22820).

q̊d (e.g.: Brit. Mus., Reg. 6 A v; Cambridge, Corp. Christi 192; Berne 292). This is really a shortening by use of the 'quo' symbol.

q̊đ (e.g. Berne 292; Cologne 113; St Omer 168; Trèves, Dom. 136).

quomodo. This word is frequently shortened by use of the 'quo' symbol or the 'modo' symbol. Or of both (q̊m̊), e.g.: [Vienna 1247]; Cologne 53 and 113; Berne 207 (Fleury); Boulogne 90 (Anglosaxon).

The peculiarly Insular symbol is however still qm̄o. It is found also in Breton MSS. In Continental script it may be said to be due to Insular influence, e.g.: Paris 12296 (Corbie); Basel F v 33 (Fulda); Autun 15.

The syllabic suspension (qm̄d) is now very rare. An example is Berne 207 (Fleury; sometimes qmd̃). This M.S. shews the derivative contraction (qmd̃o), which occurs also in Paris 1761 and Basel F v 33 and, with the addition of a suprascript *o* over the *q*, in Trèves, Stadtbibl. 170.

quoniam. The use of the ancient syllabic suspension (qn̄) is now very rare, probably owing to its possible confusion with 'quando.' It is one of the forms used in Brit. Mus., Add. 24142 (on f. 108ᵛ).

The three-letter suspension (quō) is fairly frequent in Anglosaxon script and in Insular centres on the Continent. It is the sole symbol of Düsseldorf D 1. It is fairly common in conjunction with the two-letter contraction (qm̄), e.g. in: Cassel theol. F 25 (Anglosaxon); Frankfort, St Barthol. 32 (Anglosaxon); Cambridge, Corp. Christi 389 (Anglosaxon); Leyden 88 (from Irish exemplar); Laon 135 and 136; the Anglosaxon Lambeth 149 (ff. 1–138); Berne 128 and 772; Basel B i 6 and O iv 17 (Anglosaxon); St Gall 7; Stuttgart H. B. vii 29; Trèves, Dom. 136; Cologne 53; Düsseldorf B 80; Manchester, Rylands 7. In Brit. Mus., Add. 11852 quō is usual, qm̄ rare. And quō occurs along with the confusing symbol qūm (liable to be misread as 'quum') in Laon 50, and with both qūm and qm̄ in Valenciennes 195 (Anglosaxon). In Boulogne 90 (Anglosaxon), Paris 12296 (Corbie) and Munich 13038 (Ratisbon) we find quō, qm̄, qn̄m.

The two-letter contraction (qm̄) is by far the commonest symbol in our period, and many scribes use no other. It is the sole symbol in all Irish, Welsh, Breton and Beneventan script.

The three-letter contraction (qn̄m) remains in the hands of Anglosaxon and Continental scribes. Visigothic also uses it. The only examples noted of its exclusive use in any MS. are Lambeth 414 (Canterbury) and Lambeth 325. But it occurs:

Along with quō and qm̄ in Boulogne 90 (Anglosaxon); Paris 12296 (Corbie); Munich 13038.

With qn̄ and qm̄ in: Brit. Mus., Add. 24142 (qn̄ on f. 108ᵛ).

With qm̄ in: St Omer 342 bis (qn̄m frequent, qm̄ sometimes); Laon 97 and 122 and 265; Cambridge, Corp. Christi 307 (Anglosaxon) and 279; Manchester, Rylands 83 and 104 (both Visigothic); Madrid, Bibl. Nac. 10007 (Visigothic).

In Rome, Vitt. Eman., Sess. 45 (Nonantola) a cross-stroke is sometimes put through the shaft of the q in qm̄. And on f. 229^r qño seems to denote 'quoniam' in the sentence: 'facit Deus suos spiritos angelos qño per ipsos nuntiat nobis voluntatem suam... ministri autem sunt qño illi assistunt.'

quoque. Practically all the statements made under this heading in 'Notae Latinae' (p. 269) still hold good for our period. The abbreviation of 'quoque' is still mainly confined to Insular script and the script of Continental centres under Insular influence, although it does not appear to have been quite unused in Italy. In our period too the prevalent ancient Nota (qq̄) is generally employed, the stroke being sometimes placed below (traversing the two shafts) instead of above. And the word is often written with use of the 'quo' symbol or a 'que' symbol or of both. The statement that, when the stroke is above, it either covers both letters or (more usually) stands over the second only, still holds good.

Some Continental examples of qq with stroke above are: Basel F v 33; St Gall 260; Paris 12296 (Corbie); Laon 428; Berne 28; Rome, Vitt. Eman., Sess. 44 (Nonantola; a great variety of fórms). In Cologne 113 are many forms, even the stroke both above and below the qq. And in Cologne 143, where the stroke is below, for the second q is substituted the 'que' symbol (q'). Similarly in Berne 207, where the stroke is below, the 'quo' symbol (q̊) is substituted for the first q. True instances of qq with stroke below are found (along with the form with stroke above) in: Berne 363 (Irish); Cambridge Ff iv 32 (Welsh); Basel O iv 17 (Anglosaxon); Brit. Mus., Cotton Otho E xiii (Breton); Paris 3182 (Breton).

quot. The contraction (qt̄) is still used in Insular script, though apparently not very frequently. The only examples we have noted are:

(Irish) Berne 363; the Macdurnan Gospels,
(Welsh) Cambridge, Corp. Christi 153,
(Cornish?) Oxford, Bodl. 572,
(Anglosaxon) Frankfort, St Barthol. 32,
(Breton?) Berne 207,
(Continental) Berne 87; Oxford, Bodl. 828; Brit. Mus., Add. 11852 (St Gall). The symbol (q̊) of 'quo' is often used, followed by t.

reliqua (see 'cetera ').

42 SUPPLEMENT

res. The ancient Nota (r͞r) for 'rerum' is preserved in the late Welsh script of the [Ricemarch MSS.], [Cambridge, Corp. Christi 199] and the Dublin [Ricemarch Psalter], and in the late Irish of Oxford, Bodl., [Rawl. B 502].

No trace has been found of an abbreviation of 'rebus.'

respondeo. The only part of the word now commonly abbreviated seems to be the third person singular (present or perfect). The forms are still very varied, e.g.:

r͞p in the [Book of Deer] (Irish),
r͞p and re͞p in Oxford, Laud. lat. 26 (Breton),
res͞p in Basel O IV 17 (Anglosaxon),
res͞p and rs͞p in St Omer 765.

Other shortenings are res͞pdit in Oxford, Laud. lat. 26, rep͞dit in Munich 6262 (on f. 37ʳ), r͞s and rs͞pdt in the Visigothic Brit. Mus., Add. 25600. The last writes rsp͞ndrt for the plural 'responderunt.'

saeculum. The two sets of symbols (sc͞lm, sc͞li, etc., sec͞lm, sec͞li, etc.) are still used, the former extensively. Irish script avoids any abbreviation of this word, though sc͞li occurs in Cambridge, St John's, Southampton Psalter, and Leyden 67 D and Cambridge, Corp. Christi 279 use sc͞lm.

Some examples of the first set are:

(Anglosaxon) Boulogne 90; Cambridge, Corp. Christi 307; Cassel theol. F 25; Basel O IV 17 (Anglosaxon of Fulda); Lambeth 149 (ff. 1—138); and Frankfort, St Barthol. 32,

(Cornish?) Oxford, Bodl. 572,

(Welsh) Cambridge Ff IV 32; [Cambridge, Corp. Christi 199]; the [Ricemarch Psalter],

(Breton) Cambridge, Corp. Christi 192; Brit. Mus., Cotton Otho E XIII; Paris 3182,

(Continental) Paris 12052 (Corbie); Autun 15 and 17ᴬ and 22; St Omer 168; Laon 122; Cologne 53 and 143; Düsseldorf B 80 and D 1; Trèves, Dom. 136; Stuttgart H. B. VII 29; Brit. Mus., Add. 11852 and 22820 and Harl. 3017, and Cotton Titus D XXVII; Berne 87 and 128 and 292; Basel B IV 12; Rome, Vitt. Eman., Sess. 44 (Nonantola); Lambeth 204 and 237 (ff.146-208) and 325 and 431 (ff. 145-160),

(Beneventan) Paris 335; Rome, Vitt. Eman., Sess. 56,

(Visigothic) Manchester, Rylands 83, 89 and 104; Brit. Mus.,

Add. 30852; Madrid, Bibl. Nac. 10007; Madrid, Bibl. Acad. Hist. 24 and 10067.

Of the second: Paris 12296 (Corbie); Munich 6262; St Omer 33 bis; Berne 207; Hague 5.

Both sets are occasionally used, e.g.: Trèves, Stadtbibl. 169; Paris 1761; Brussels 10470-3; Munich 13038; St Gall 7; Rome, Vitt. Eman., Sess. 71.

For 'saecularis' we find sclaris, e.g.: in the Breton Brit. Mus., Cotton Otho E XIII; in the Beneventan Paris 335; in the Visigothic Manchester, Rylands 83 and 89; also in Trèves, Stadtbibl. 170; Cambridge Ee II 4; Berne 236.

In the Visigothic Manchester, Rylands 104 and Madrid, Bibl. Acad. Hist. 24 we find the forms slarii and slaris respectively. These forms are based on the slm, sli, etc., found in Anglosaxon script earlier than our period. No examples of the simple forms slm, sli, etc., have been noted in our period.

scilicet. The rare persistence of the initial suspension (s· or s̄) may be mentioned, e.g.: Munich 13038; Rome, Vitt. Eman., Sess. 45 (Nonantola).

secundum. Irish, Welsh and occasionally Anglosaxon script still preserve the Insular symbol (minuscule s with a stroke through the descending shaft); sometimes the endings 'm,' 'um,' 'i,' 'di,' etc., are added to distinguish the adjectival forms. Anglosaxon examples are: Brit. Mus., Cotton Vitell. C VIII; Boulogne 90 (on f. 104ʳ). A Cornish (?) is Oxford, Bodl. 572 (also scđm and scđum).

The Continental syllabic suspension (scđ or sēd) persists in such MSS. as: Boulogne 90 (Anglosaxon; also scđs, scđam, scđus); Basel F v 33 (Fulda; also scđm); Munich 13038 (also sēcd, scđm); Brit. Mus., Add. 11852 (also scđm, secđm, secđ); Paris 3182 (Breton; also secđa, scđm, secđm, sed̄). But nowhere is it the sole symbol. Far more common are the two contractions (scđm, secđm), particularly the former. In 'Notae Latinae' (p. 279) is suggested that the form secđm may be either a more precise form of scđ or due to the use of the 'cum' and 'dum' symbols. May not this form and the scđm variety have been influenced by the two similar 'saeculum' symbols, seclm and sclm? At any rate there seems to be some relationship between the symbolism of the two words. In Continental script it is true to say that a scribe who writes scđm will always use the form scĩm only. The contrary is not so invariably true. A scribe who writes scĩm will generally write scđm, though he may use the two 'secundum' forms concurrently, as in: Brit. Mus., Add. 1185 and 22820; Berne 128 and 167 and 236; Paris 3182. Exceptions to this rule are: Paris 335 (Beneventan) and 3182 (Breton); Berne 87, etc.; all of these use the scĩm and secđm forms side by side. Generally speaking however, if both scĩm and secĩm occur in a MS., then secđm and scđm are found also, e.g.: St Omer 33 bis; Brussels 10470-3; St Gall 7; Rome, Vitt. Eman., Sess. 71. Sometimes the more precise form is written simply secđ, e.g. Brit. Mus., Add. 24142.

Beneventan script still favours this precise form.

The secund forms are of course not true abbreviations, but examples of the use of the syllable-suspension '-um.'

The occurrence of the scđm, etc., forms is very frequent; and mostly these symbols are the sole ones employed, as in the following MSS.: Brussels 1370; [Vienna 1247]; Autun 15 and 17ᴬ and 122; St Omer 342 bis and 765; Laon 97 and 135 and 136 and 468; Paris 1761 and 12052 and 12296; Cologne 53 and 113 and 143; Trèves, Dom. 136; Trèves, Stadtbibl. 170; Leyden 67 D and 88; Rome, Vitt. Eman., Sess. 44 and 45; Berne 207 and 292; Cambridge, Corp. Christi 307; Lambeth 200; Brit. Mus., Harl. 3017 and Reg. 6 A v and Cotton Titus D xxvii; Oxford, Laud. lat. 26; Manchester, Rylands 7; the Breton MS., Brit. Mus., Cotton Otho E xiii; the Visigothic MSS., Madrid, Bibl. Acad. Hist. 24 and 25 and 10067, and Bibl. Nac. 10007.

The following are examples of MSS. using the scđm, etc., forms along with varieties (other than secđm, etc.): Basel F v 33 (also scđ); Oxford, Bodl. 572 (also scđum and the Insular symbol); Autun 45 (also sđm on f. 82ʳ); Boulogne 90 (also scđus, scđ and the Insular symbol).

Examples of MSS. using the secđm, etc., forms are: Paris 335 (Beneventan); Glasgow, v 3. 2 (Beneventan); Berne 172; St Gall 46; Munich 6262; Hague 5; Brussels 10470-3 (also scđm, etc.); Brit. Mus., Add. 22820 (also scđm, etc.); Rome, Vitt. Eman., Sess. 71; Berne 128 and 236 (also scđm, etc.); St Gall 7; St Omer 33 bis (also secđ, scđm); Berne 167 (also scđm, sđm); [Leyden 118] (Beneventan; also scđs); Brit. Mus., Cotton Vesp. A viii (also scđm); Brit. Mus., Add. 11852 (also scđm, scđ); Valenciennes 195 (Anglosaxon); Basel B ɪ 6; Paris 3182 (also scđm, scđ); Manchester, Rylands 98 (also scđm, secđ); the Anglosaxon Lambeth 149 (ff. 1–138; also scđm).

The three-letter suspension (seč) survives in: Frankfort, St Barthol. 32 (Anglosaxon); Trèves, Stadtbibl. 122, etc.

sed. The Insular symbol (*s* in this or in minuscule form, with a stroke above) remains the sole symbol in Insular MSS. It is never found in Continental script unless under Insular influence.

Continental scribes use minuscule *s* with a comma (generally placed low down), e.g.: Autun 45; Paris 1761; Berne 128 and 207; Brit. Mus., Add. 11852; Stuttgart H. B. vɪɪ 29; Cologne 113.

Breton scribes still substitute a dot for the comma and add a dot on the left-hand side also, e.g. Brit. Mus., Cotton Otho E xɪɪɪ; Paris 3182; Berne 167 (also minuscule *s* with comma).

In four MSS., St Omer 765, Berne 292, Lambeth 431 (ff. 145–160), and Brit. Mus., Cotton Vesp. B vɪ (ff. 1–103), a variety (s;) was noted; and on f. 4ʳ of Rome, Vitt. Eman., Sess. 45 a transected *s*, the earlier Insular symbol (also minuscule *s* with 7-shaped comma, and on f. 25ʳ minuscule *s* with a dot on each side and a stroke above).

One example only was noted of the contraction (sđ), Berne 87 (f. 7ᵛ).

sequitur. The abbreviation of this word seems still to be very capricious. No particular form seems confined to any one area. No abbreviations of the plural 'sequuntur' have been noted.

Examples are:
(1) seq̄r Paris 12296; Laon 50 (also with stroke under the *q*); Munich 6262 (also seq̄t) and 13038 (also seqᵗt); Manchester, Rylands 83 (also sq̄r, sq̄tr).
(2) seq̄ Frankfort, St Barthol. 32; Stuttgart H. B. vɪɪ 29; St Omer 168 (also sq̄).
(3) sq̄r Manchester, Rylands 83 and 104 (the former uses seq̄r̄ and sq̄tr also).
(4) seq̄t Leyden 67 D; St Omer 33 bis; Lambeth 149 (ff. 1–138).
(5) seqtr̄, Manchester, Rylands 98 (also sqtr̄).

The word can of course be shortened by use of the 'qui' and 'ur' symbols.

sicut. The Irish and Welsh symbol ($\overset{i}{\text{s}}$) remains, though occasionally the *i* is written alongside the *s*, and appears even in Anglosaxon (e.g. Brit. Mus., Cotton Vitell. C VIII) and Breton (e.g. Cambridge, Corp. Christi 192). The Irish Berne 363 has the contraction s^t (liable to confusion with 'sunt,' as $\overset{i}{\text{s}}$ to confusion with 'sibi').

But the commonest symbol in our period is the three-letter suspension (sic̄), found in all Continental script. Sometimes a comma is substituted for the abbreviation-stroke over the *c*.

Examples of this suspension are: Oxford, Bodl. 572 (Cornish?); Cassel theol. F 25 (Anglosaxon); Frankfort, St Barthol. 32 (Anglosaxon); Cambridge, Corp. Christi 307 (Anglosaxon); Cambridge Ee II 4; Brit. Mus., Add. 11852 and 22820, and Harl. 3017, and Cotton Tib. A II; Vienna 1247; Autun 15 and 31 and 45; Épinal 78; Valenciennes 195 (Anglosaxon); St Omer 765; Laon 135 and 136 and 428; Brussels 10470–3; Paris 1761 and 3182 and 12052; Lambeth 149 (ff. 1–138) and 237 (ff. 146–208) and 431; Cologne 53 and 113; Trèves, Stadtbibl. 122 and 170; Stuttgart H. B. VII 29; Munich 6262; Berne 128 and 167; Basel B IV 12 and B I 6; Rome, Vitt. Eman., Sess. 44 (Nonantola); Paris 335 (Beneventan).

Examples of the comma substituted are: Rome, Vitt. Eman., Sess. 45 (also sic̄); St Gall 7 (also sic̄); Berne 207 (also sic̄); St Omer 33 bis; Laon 265; Berne 236; Lambeth 200.

The contraction (sic̄t) based on the suspension is found in: Berne 292; Brit. Mus., Cotton Otho E XIII (Breton; also sic̄); [Leyden 118] (Beneventan; also sic̄). It is possibly a mere substitution of the abbreviation-stroke for a suprascript *u*.

similiter. This word is rarely symbolized, and nothing approaching a recognised symbol is found. The following may be called capricious forms:

simiłt Autun 31,
simił Trèves, Stadtbibl. 170,
simłit Basel B I 6,
smłr Berne 207.

sine. The syllabic suspension (sn̄) persists in Irish and Welsh MSS. It appears too on f. 83^r of the Anglosaxon Boulogne 90, but here it denotes the imperative of 'sino,' not the preposition.

sive. The similar suspension (sū), so easily confused with 'sum,' is now characteristic of Welsh and Irish MSS., though not so commonly found as sn̄ 'sine.' It appears too in the Anglosaxon Boulogne 90. In the Cornish (?) Oxford, Bodl. 572, which uses sic̄ 'sicut' and s̄ 'sed,' the form s̓ is used for 'sive'; so also in the late Irish [Book of Deer], which uses s̓ for 'sicut' too (along with sī and sic̄) and s̄ 'sed.'

Confusion of all these symbols (and of s̓ 'sibi') must occur sometimes. Two MSS. given to Strasbourg Cathedral by bishop Erkanbald (of 965–991) employ sū 'sive,' Basel B ɪ 6 and B ɪv 12.

Spiritus (see 'Christus').

sunt. The 'Insular' symbol (s̄t) is still entitled to its name, in that it is the only symbol found in Irish, Welsh and Anglosaxon script. (One occurrence of the Continental symbol s̄ occurs on f. 83ʳ of the Anglosaxon Lambeth 149.) It is also the commonest form in Beneventan. But its use on the Continent appears to be growing; for example, it is the sole symbol in such MSS. as: Manchester, Rylands 7 (Prüm); Brit. Mus., Cotton Tib. A ɪɪ; Trèves, Stadtbibl. 122; Berne 292; St Gall 19; Rome, Vitt. Eman., Sess. 44 (Nonantola). And it is used along with the Continental symbol (s̄) in such MSS. as: Laon 50 and 136 and 265 and 468; Épinal 78 (usually s̄); Cologne 53 (rarely s̄) and 113; Trèves, Stadtbibl. 170; [Vienna 1247]; Munich 13038; Brit. Mus., Add. 11852 and 24142; St Gall 260; Berne 87 and 167 and 236; Basel F v 33; Rome, Vitt. Eman., Sess. 45 (Nonantola) and 56 (Beneventan); [Leyden 118] (Beneventan); Paris 3182 (Breton); Brit. Mus., Cotton Otho E xɪɪɪ (Breton).

Examples of the Continental (s̄) as sole symbol are: Autun 15 and 17ᴬ and 22 and 31 and 45; St Omer 33 bis and 765; Laon 97 and 428; Paris 1761 and 12052 and 12296; Trèves, Dom. 136; Stuttgart H. B. vɪɪ 29; Munich 6262; St Gall 7 (the fourth scribe substitutes an apostrophe for the abbreviation-stroke); Berne 128 and 169 and 172 and 207; Basel B ɪ 6 and B ɪv 12; Cambridge, Corp. Christi 223 and 279; Oxford, Bodl. 828; Brit. Mus., Add. 22820 and Harl. 3017; Lambeth 325, 427, and 431 (ff. 145–160).

Visigothic scribes still write the word in full or employ the device of writing suprascript *n* by means of an abbreviation-stroke (sūt).

super. The contraction (s̄r) remains an Irish and Welsh symbol, e.g.:

(Irish) Berne 363 (also s̄rior 'superior,' s̄ruis 'supervis' for 'superbis'),

(Welsh) Cambridge Ff IV 32 (also s̄rba 'superba').

The word can of course be shortened by use of the 'per' symbol.

supra. The three-letter suspension (sup̄) has been noted in: Paris 12296 (Corbie): Autun 17^A (margin); Épinal 78; [Leyden 118] (Beneventan). And (properly 'supera') the Insular s̄ra in the Macdurnan Gospels and the [Book of Deer].

But more often the word is shortened by use of a 'ra' symbol. For example, suṗ appears in Autun 45; Brit. Mus., Cotton Titus D XXVII; Add. 11852 and 22820; Rome, Vitt. Eman., Sess. 44. And with two commas substituted for the suprascript *a* in the Irish Berne 363.

suprascriptus. In Trèves, Stadtbibl. 170 sstus has been noted.

suus (see 'meus').

tamen, tantum. It is convenient to treat these two words together, since the two commonest symbols, both of them contractions (tñ 'tamen,' tm̄ 'tantum'), generally occur side by side. They are essentially Insular (and Breton) symbols, found also in Continental centres under Insular influence. Continental examples are: Berne 207 (Breton?) and 263; Leyden 88 (under Irish influence); Munich 6262.

Confusion inevitably arises between these two words, owing to the occasional use of the syllabic suspension (tm̄) for 'tamen,' a suspension identical with the contraction (tm̄) for 'tantum.' This misleading suspension occurs, e.g., in: Munich 13038; Berne 167 (Breton; in a marginal comment); Laon 50 (f. 3^v). The last MS. uses tñ elsewhere for 'tamen'!

The word 'tamen' can of course be shortened by use of the 'en' symbol; and this shortening is extremely common (tam̄), e.g.: [Vienna 1247]; Brussels 10470–3; Laon 135.

tempore. The two ancient Notae (temp̄, tp̄r) still exist, the former, e.g., in; St Omer 342 bis. The latter, e.g., in: Cologne 113; Munich 6262; Rome, Vitt. Eman., Sess. 44 and 45.

But a variety (temp̄r) or with the abbreviation-stroke and 'm'-stroke united (tep̄r) is still the most universal symbol. Examples

of the former are: Épinal 78; Manchester, Rylands 7 (also temp̄,
tep̄); Boulogne 90 (also temp̄re); Munich 13038 (also temp̄re);
Cologne 53; Trèves, Dom. 136; Brit. Mus., Cotton Otho E xɪɪɪ and
Cotton Titus D xxvɪɪ (also tpr̄e); Lambeth 149 (ff. 1–138) and 204
(also tep̄r); Berne 128; Basel B ɪ 6 and F v 33; St Gall 7; Rome,
Vitt. Eman., Sess. 71 (also tep̄r); [Leyden 118] (with suprascript
m). Of the latter: Brit. Mus., Cotton Tib. A ɪɪ; Autun 31 and 45;
St Omer 33 bis and 342 bis (also temp̄, tep̄, temp̄r); Paris 12052;
Laon 135; Düsseldorf B 80; Trèves, Stadtbibl. 170; Rome, Vitt.
Eman., Sess. 44 and 45. This last MS. has tēpr̄e, tp̄r, tp̄re also. The
form tempō is found in Cambridge Ff ɪv 32 and in [Oxford, Bodl.,
Rawl. B 502].

It is noteworthy that in abbreviations of the oblique cases of
'tempus' other than the Ablative the final vowel always figures,
e.g. tēpr̄a, Trèves, Stadtbibl. 169; tpr̄a, Rome, Vitt. Eman., Sess. 44
and 45; tēpa, Rome, Vitt. Eman., Sess. 44; tēp̄ris, Leyden 67 D
and Trèves, Stadtbibl. 170; tēpīs and tēpī, Berne 363.

ter (see the Syllable-symbol 'er').

tibi (see 'mihi').

trans. No trace has been found of the three-letter contraction
(tr̄s) in our period, though one scribe (on f. 1ʳ) of Cambridge Ff ɪv
32 uses the strange form tñs. The two-letter contraction (ts̄) remains the symbol in Insular script:

(Irish) Berne 363; Leyden 67 D and 88,
(Welsh) Cambridge Ff ɪv 32 (f. 46ᵛ); Cambridge, Corp. Christi
153 (f. 16ᵛ),
(Anglosaxon) Boulogne 90 (f. 92ʳ ts̄igi 'transigi'); Brit. Mus.,
Cotton Vitell. C vɪɪɪ.

tunc (see 'nunc').

tuus (see 'meus').

vel. No occurrences of the oldest symbol (ū) have been noted in
our period except those on f. 1 of the Welsh Cambridge Ff ɪv 32
and on f. 18ʳ of Berne 236.

The two usual symbols (ul and ł) are both still of frequent occurrence. Insular script still admits only the second (though the
Anglosaxon Lambeth 149 is an exception, admitting both ł and ul);
also such Continental MSS. as Brussels 10470–3; Hague 5; Leyden
88; Autun 17ᴬ; Épinal 78; St Omer 168; Laon 50 and 265 and

464; Brit. Mus., Cotton Vesp. B VI; Cologne 113; Düsseldorf
D 1; Munich 6262; Stuttgart H. B. VII 29; Berne 87 and 88 and
167 and 207; Basel B I 6; Paris 1761; Lambeth 237 (ff. 146–208).
Beneventan MSS. still use only the Continental form (uł), though
[Leyden 118] uses both. Visigothic MSS. too still confine them-
selves to the Continental form.

But in most Continental script both forms occur side by side,
e.g.: Autun 15 and 31 and 45; Laon 135 and 136 and 428 and 468;
Cologne 53 and 143; Trèves, Dom. 136; Trèves, Stadtbibl. 169
and 170; Munich 13038; Cambridge Ee II 4; Cambridge, Corp.
Christi 279; Brit. Mus., Add. 22820 and 24142 and Cotton Otho
E XIII (Breton); Berne 128 and 169 and 172 and 236; St Gall 46;
Basel F v 33; Rome, Vitt. Eman., Sess. 44 and 45; Lambeth 204
and 431 (ff. 145–160).

Examples of uł as sole symbol are: Brussels 1370; Autun 22;
St Omer 33 bis; Brit. Mus., Harl. 3017 and Reg. 6 A v; Berne
292; Basel B IV 12; Rome, Vitt. Eman., Sess. 71; Lambeth 325
and 427.

vero. The most common symbol is still the contraction (ũ), often
written with the v-form of u by Welsh and Irish scribes. It is now
almost as frequent in Continental as in Insular script. Spanish
scribes still avoid it.

Examples in Continental script are: Lambeth 431 (ff. 145–160);
Brit. Mus., Cotton Titus D XXVII; Autun 15 and 45; St Omer 33 bis
and 765; Cologne 113; Manchester, Rylands 7; Trèves, Dom.
136; Trèves, Stadtbibl. 169 and 170; Stuttgart H. B. VII 29;
Munich 6262 and 13038; Cambridge Ee II 4; Cambridge, Corp.
Christi 223; Brit. Mus., Harl. 3017 and Reg. 6 A v; Berne 88 and
167 and 207 and 292; Paris 1761 and 12296. Of Beneventan
Lowe (Loew) 'Beneventan Script' (p. 196) says: "Not common
before saec. xi."

The other symbol (ũo), where the 'er' symbol is employed, also
occurs, but not frequently, e.g.: the Southampton Psalter (Irish);
Leyden 67 D (under Irish influence); Rome, Vitt. Eman., Sess. 56
(Beneventan); Autun 31; Hague 5; St Gall 7 and 260.

Both ũ and ũo appear e.g. in: Leyden 88 (ũ rare); Berne 128;
Rome, Vitt. Eman., Sess. 44 and 45; [Leyden 118] (Beneventan).
And any scribe who habitually writes ũ 'ver' may write ũa

'vera,' etc., e.g. Boulogne 90 (Anglosaxon); [Leyden 118] (Beneventan).

vesper. Noteworthy is vesp̄m 'vesperum' in the Beneventan [Leyden 118].

vester (see 'noster').

vobis (see 'nobis').

unde. The suspension (uñ) is still a feature of Irish and Welsh script. It occurs also in the Anglosaxon Boulogne 90, the Cornish (?) Oxford, Bodl. 572, etc. Also e.g. in: Rome, Vitt. Eman., Sess. 44 and 45 (Nonantola); [Leyden 118] (Beneventan). The shortening unđ (e.g. Cologne 153) employs the syllable-symbol '-e'.

usque. Characteristic of our period (and later) is the fairly common suspension (us̄) in Insular script, e.g.:

(Irish) the Southampton Psalter; [Oxford, Bodl., Rawl. B 502]; the [Book of Deer],

(Welsh) Cambridge, Corp. Christi 153 and [199]; the [Ricemarch Psalter],

(Anglosaxon) Boulogne 90.

ut. Characteristic too of our period, or rather later, is the suprascript *t*-form (ů) in Irish and Welsh, e.g.:

(Irish) [Oxford, Bodl., Rawl. B 502]; the [Book of Deer],

(Welsh) the [Ricemarch MSS.], Cambridge, Corp. Christi 199 and the Psalter at Dublin,

(Cornish?) Oxford, Bodl. 572 (the sole symbol).

But the 'Welsh' symbol (v̇ or v̊) spreads from Welsh MSS. to late Irish ([Oxford, Bodl., Rawl. B 502]; the [Book of Deer]) and Anglosaxon (Boulogne 90).

SYLLABLE- AND LETTER-SYMBOLS

con-. The reversed *c* (ɔ) is still the Insular symbol, and the 'cum' symbol (c̄) is still used by Continental scribes. The Insular symbol is undoubtedly due to Insular influence in such MSS. as: Cambridge, Corp. Christi 279; Laon 50; Munich 6262. The two symbols are found together in such MSS. as: Leyden 67 D; Cambridge, Corp. Christi 389; Berne 167 and 236.

Breton scribes (e.g. Cambridge, Corp. Christi 192; Brit. Mus., Cotton Otho E xiii; Paris 3182) generally use the Continental form. So does Beneventan script (e.g. [Leyden 118]; Glasgow v 3. 2; Rome, Vitt. Eman., Sess. 56).

-e. The symbolism of final *e* is rarely found in our period except after *d*; Manchester, Rylands 7 has nomiñ 'nomine" on f. 44ʳ. In Boulogne 90 (Anglosaxon) ñ denotes '-ne' on f. 73ᵛ, but elsewhere '-nem.' In Berne 167 we find nat̄ 'nate'; in Berne 207 ecc̄ 'ecce' and q̊r̄ 'quare'; in Paris 12052 miserer̄ 'miserere.'

A horizontal stroke through the shaft of *d* is still a fairly common method of representing '-de,' e.g. und̄ 'unde' in: Paris 1761 and 12296; Cologne 153; Stuttgart H. B. vii 29; Berne 167 and 207. So in the Visigothic Madrid, Bibl. Nac. 10007 and 10041. Berne 207 (Fleury) sometimes writes uñd 'unde' as well as ind̄ 'inde.'

-em. This syllable is found abbreviated after *d* and *n* in our period, but practically only in Insular script or Insular centres.

The old form, with horizontal stroke just to the right of the consonant, occurs e.g. in:

(Welsh) Cambridge, Corp. Christi 153 ('-dem'); Cambridge Ff iv 32 ('-nem'); the [Ricemarch Psalter] ('-dem,' '-nem'),

(Irish) the Macdurnan Gospels ('-nem'); the Southampton Psalter ('-nem'); [Oxford, Bodl., Rawl. B 502] ('-dem').

The more common forms are, however, *d* with cross-stroke through the shaft (d̄), *n* with abbreviation-stroke above (ñ). Examples of d̄ '-dem' are: Brit. Mus., Cotton Otho E xiii (Breton; q̊d̄ 'quidem'); Cotton Titus D xxvii eid̄ 'eiusdem'; Berne 167 (with Breton glosses; quid̄ 'quidem'); Paris 12052 (Corbie; eund̄ 'eundem'); St Omer 342bis (eund 'eundem'); Autun 15 (eiusd 'eiusdem'). Examples of ñ '-nem': Boulogne 90 (Anglosaxon); Brit. Mus., Cotton Otho E xiii (Breton).

Also m̄ '-mem' occurs in Brussels 1370. But its use for the first syllable of 'membrum' (e.g. Leyden 67 D; Berne 292; Autun 17ᴬ; Rome, Vitt. Eman., Sess. 44; Épinal 78) may rather be the 'en' symbol and reflect a spelling 'menbrum.' Similarly nom̄i 'nomini' (e.g. on f. 9ᵛ of Munich 6262), and the like, rather are due to the m̄ '-men' of the nominative nom̄ 'nomen.' And aut̄ 'autem' (q.v.) is rather an expansion of the old suspension aū 'autem' than the use of the '-em' symbol.

en. The use of the symbol (m̄) to denote 'men-' (e.g. 'mensa'), '-men-' (e.g. 'immensus'), '-men' (e.g. 'tamen,' 'nomen') is now practically universal, except in Visigothic script, though two Visigothic MSS., Manchester, Rylands 89 and Brit. Mus., Add. 25600, use am̄ 'amen.' The final syllable is most often symbolized (the principle of suspension also comes into play here), especially in 'tamen' and 'nomen.'

Examples for final 'men' in Insular script are:

(Anglosaxon) Boulogne 90; Cambridge, Corp. Christi 307 and 389; Cassel theol. F 25; Lambeth 149 (ff. 1–138),

(Irish) the Macdurnan Gospels; Leyden 67 D; the Southampton Psalter, the [Book of Deer],

(Welsh) Cambridge Ff iv 32; Cambridge, Corp. Christi 153 and [199]; the [Ricemarch Psalter],

(Cornish?) Oxford, Bodl. 572.

And for medial 'men':

(Anglosaxon) Exeter Charter 2519 (of 938) and 2526 (of 1044),

(Irish) the Macdurnan Gospels,

(Welsh) the [Ricemarch Psalter].

Examples of the symbolism of initial 'men' are:

Frankfort, St Barthol. 32 (Anglosaxon of Fulda); Trèves, Dom. 136; Autun 15 and 45; Berne 236; Rome, Vitt. Eman., Sess. 71.

er. The symbol (t̄) for the syllable 'ter' is very common for the final syllable; it is also used (but far less frequently) for the initial and medial occurrences of the syllable. No examples however of this syllable-symbol have been noted in Visigothic script of our period. All other scripts use it frequently.

Occasionally a comma is substituted for the abbreviation-stroke, e.g. in: St Gall 90; Frankfort, St Barthol. 32 (sometimes); Rome, Vitt. Eman., Sess. 45 (on f. 49ʳ). The Beneventan [Leyden 118] substitutes a 3-mark, and the Beneventan Paris 335 a 2-mark. This use of the comma and the 2- (or 3-) mark makes confusion with 'tur' possible.

A similar symbol (ū) for the syllable 'ver' is fairly generally used. This symbol stands indifferently for any position of the syllable. It is however not nearly so frequent as the 'ter' symbol. Examples are:

(Anglosaxon) Lambeth 218,

(Irish) the Macdurnan Gospels; Leyden 67 D,

(Welsh) Cambridge Ff ɪv 32; Cambridge, Corp. Christi 153 and [199] (both with ūū 'verum'),

(Cornish?) Oxford, Bodl. 572,

(Beneventan) Rome, Vitt. Eman., Sess. 56; [Leyden 118] (also with the 2-mark for the abbreviation-stroke),

(Continental) Brit. Mus., Add. 11852; Brit. Mus., Cotton Vesp. A vɪɪɪ; Cambridge, Corp. Christi 192; Cologne 53 and 113; Autun 15 and 22 and 31; St Omer 168 and 765; Trèves, Stadtbibl. 169; Stuttgart H. B. vɪɪ 29; St Gall 7; Berne 167 and 169; Rome, Vitt. Eman., Sess. 44 and 45; Manchester, Rylands 7.

Isolated instances only have been noted of the following analogous syllable-symbols:

ñ 'ner' in [Leyden 118] (Beneventan; 'genera'),

đ 'der' in Berne 292; [Leyden 118],

c̄ 'cer' in Rome, Vitt. Eman., Sess. 45; Berne 292.

The 'ber' syllable-symbol (ƀ), initial, medial or final, has been left till last, so that it can precede discussion of the 'bis' syllable. For usually the same symbol denotes both, 'ber' and 'bis'; though in the Irish Macdurnan Gospels the 'ber' syllable is written with the abbreviation-stroke to the right of the shaft of the b, whereas the stroke for 'bis' is on top of the shaft, just touching and crossing it; similarly in Berne 128. Examples of ƀ 'ber' or 'bis' are: Leyden 67 D (Irish); Oxford, Bodl. 572 (Cornish?); Brussels 10470-3; Leyden 21; Brit. Mus., Add. 11852 and Cotton Titus D xxvɪɪ; Paris 1761; Autun 15 and 17ᴬ and 45; Cologne 53; Stuttgart H. B. vɪɪ 29; St Gall 7; Berne 167 and 169 and 236 and 292; Rome,

Vitt. Eman., Sess. 44 and 45 and 71; Lambeth 325 and 431 (ff. 145-160).

Generally speaking, any MS. that uses Ƀ 'ber' shews Ƀ 'bis' (largely owing to the almost universal occurrence of noƀ 'nobis,' uoƀ 'vobis').

is. By far the commonest final syllable shewing the 'is' abbreviation is Ƀ 'bis.' In addition to the examples just given where this symbol denotes both 'ber' and 'bis,' these MSS. may be mentioned for Ƀ '-bis':

(Continental) Lambeth 204 and 427; Leyden 88; Autun 22; St Omer 33 bis and 342 bis; Laon 122 and 135 and 136 and 265; Manchester, Rylands 7 and 98; Trèves, Stadtbibl. 169; Munich 6262 and 13038; Brit. Mus., Cotton Vesp. B VI and Cotton Tib. A II and Add. 24142; Paris 3182 and 12052 and 12296; Berne 172; Basel B I 6 and B IV 12,

(Anglosaxon) Lambeth 149 (ff. 1-138),

(Beneventan) Glasgow V 3. 2; Paris 335.

The Visigothic Manchester, Rylands 83 and 104 both shew Ƀ 'bis,' although this symbol seems rare in Spanish script. That Spanish scribes prefer a peculiar cedilla-like symbol for the 'is' of 'bis' (and 'lis,' etc.) is mentioned in 'Notae Latinae' (p. 337).

Next in frequency is probably the symbol ł '-lis,' e.g. in: [Oxford, Bodl., Rawl. B 502] (late Irish); Oxford, Laud. lat. 26; [Leyden 118] (Beneventan); Rome, Vitt. Eman., Sess. 45; Laon 468; Trèves, Stadtbibl. 170; Berne 167 and 172 and 236; Manchester, Rylands 7; Lambeth 204 and 431 (ff. 145-160). In the marginalia of Autun 22, ł occurs for '-les.'

Other 'is' syllable-symbols are:

đ '-dis' in Brit. Mus., Cotton Otho E XIII (Breton); Laon 468; Autun 15; Rome, Vitt. Eman., Sess. 45.

ḡ '-gis' in Oxford, Laud. lat. 26.

r̄ '-ris' in Rome, Vitt. Eman., Sess. 44.

The Visigothic Madrid, Bibl. Nac. 10041 writes n with subscript i̯ for '-nis.'

-it. This common final syllable is still frequently and universally abbreviated, with the same two exceptions as were found in the previous period ('Notae Latinae,' p. 340): neither Insular scribes

56 SUPPLEMENT

of home centres nor Spanish scribes use the 'it' abbreviation, with
these exceptions:

(Anglosaxon) Lambeth 149,
(Welsh) Cambridge, Corp. Christi 153,
(Irish) the Macdurnan Gospels.

The symbol is an abbreviation-stroke over the preceding consonant, a stroke that transects the shaft of the tall letters such as
d and *l*. By far the commonest syllables so abbreviated are '-cit'
and '-xit,' owing probably to the frequency of 'dicit,' 'dixit,' 'facit,'
'fecit,' etc.

The next in order of frequency is ū '-uit' (or '-vit'). Examples
are: Leyden 67 D (under Irish influence); [Leyden 118] (Beneventan); Cologne 113; Trèves, Stadtbibl. 169; Munich 6262;
Paris 3182; Berne 128 and 169; Basel O iv 17 (Anglosaxon; ů);
St Gall 19 and 46 (ů); Rome, Vitt. Eman., Sess. 45 (ú).

Other less frequent usages are:

ƀ '-bit' in Autun 15 ('dabit' f. 147ʳ; also ƀ '-bis' and 'ber');
Laon 265 (also ƀ '-bis'); Trèves, Stadtbibl. 169 (also ƀ '-bis' and
'ber'); Paris 1761; Rome, Vitt. Eman., Sess. 71 (also bī).

đ '-dit' in Leyden 67 D and 88; St Omer 168; Laon 265; Trèves,
Stadtbibl. 122 and 169; Munich 13038; Brit. Mus., Add. 11852;
Paris 1761; Berne 167; Basel B i 6; St Gall 19 and 46; Rome,
Vitt. Eman., Sess. 45.

ł '-lit' in Leyden 67 D.

ƥ '-pit' in [Leyden 118] (Beneventan); Berne 236; Basel O iv
17 (Anglosaxon). But *p* with stroke through the shaft in Trèves,
Stadtbibl. 169.

ñ '-nit' in Trèves, Stadtbibl. 169.

The Spanish 'it' ligature mentioned on page 340 of 'Notae
Latinae' may be exemplified by the Visigothic Manchester, Rylands
89 and Brit. Mus., Add. 25600 (both from S. Pedro de Cardeña).
Occasionally the vertical stroke is transected by a horizontal line.
Rylands 89 uses this ligature for both '-it' and '-ti-', e.g. dicȚ
and dicT (dicti); genTles; canTcum; propheTa; menTbus; sedT;
-sT (-sit). Brit. Mus., Add. 25600 uses it for final '-it' only, e.g.
-dT; -bT; -sT.

m. Final and medial (preconsonantal) *m* are now almost universally symbolized by means of an abbreviation-stroke written

over the preceding letter. The only examples noted in our period of the symbolism of prevocalic *m* are dōū 'domum' in the Irish Macdurnan Gospels and anīadvertione, anīadversiones 'animad-' in Autun 22. Such usage is by no means common as yet.

Sometimes the abbreviation-stroke is placed through the shaft of the nearest tall letter (as quiđa, quiđe in Autun 17ᴬ and Paris 12296), or receded to the nearest consonant (as eñi 'enim' in Berne 167). Visigothic script often puts a dot above the abbreviation-stroke (e.g. Manchester, Rylands 83 and 104), or a dot above two abbreviation-strokes (as in Brit. Mus., Add. 30852; where the *n*-stroke has no dot). The Beneventan Glasgow v 3. 2 uses a comma instead of an abbreviation-stroke, though one scribe writes suprascript *m* by the 3-mark. This 3-mark is used also by the Beneventan Rome, Vitt. Eman., Sess. 56. A suprascript *s*-mark, placed to the right of the final or medial vowel, is used in the Anglosaxon Cassel theol. F 25 and Lambeth 200. Insular scribes affect a hooked form of the horizontal abbreviation-stroke.

n. This letter is not nearly so often symbolized by an abbreviation-stroke as is *m*. The only examples of final *n* so treated occur in the words 'non,' 'in,' 'con-.'

Occasionally a sign resembling *N* written on its side or approaching the Greek minuscule Xi (ξ) is used instead of the horizontal stroke (e.g. in MSS. of Laon). Visigothic scribes often add a dot above the abbreviation-stroke or double it.

Medial *n* is found symbolized in such words as:

mōs 'mons' in Laon 97 and 135.

tātum 'tantum' in St Omer 168.

frequēter 'frequenter' in Trèves, Stadtbibl. 169.

līquens 'linquens' in Berne 172.

fūdū 'fundum' in Berne 236.

hīc 'hinc' in the Welsh [Cambridge, Corp. Christi 199].

gētis 'gentis' and volūtate 'voluntate' in Brit. Mus., Cotton Vesp. A VIII.

And Spanish MSS. in particular abound in the symbolism of medial preconsonantal *n*, e.g. 'sunt,' '-runt,' '-ens,' 'quando,' etc. They also frequently use the symbol for final *n* in the word 'non.' Beneventan MSS. also use nō 'non' (e.g. Paris 335; Glasgow v 3. 2).

Commoner even than nō 'non' is ī 'in,' though this latter is
still largely confined to Insular script and in Continental script
may mostly be due to Insular influence. Continental examples
are: Cambridge Ee II 4; Berne 167; Brit. Mus., Cotton Titus D
XXVII; Cologne 53. Breton examples are: Paris 3182; Brit. Mus.,
Cotton Otho E XIII. In Beneventan too, e.g. [Leyden 118]; Lowe
(Loew) 'Beneventan Script' (p. 184) says of it: "Is used saec. xi
in. to saec. xiv. Typical of recent MSS."

The Visigothic Manchester, Rylands 89 shews I with cross-stroke
for the syllable 'in' of both 'intellegit' and 'inter.'

Quite unique in our period (for it is really a later usage) is the
symbolism of prevocalic *n* in the Breton Brit. Mus., Cotton Otho
E XIII (testimōi).

or. After the letter *f* and in Insular MSS., mainly Welsh and
Irish, 'or' is denoted by an abbreviation-stroke, apparently from
about the year 900. Examples are:

(Irish) the Macdurnan Gospels ('forte,' 'fornicatio'); [Oxford,
Bodl., Rawl. B 502]; the [Book of Deer] ('forte,' 'foras,' 'foris'),

(Welsh) [Cambridge, Corp. Christi 199] ('foris'); the [Ricemarch
Psalter] ('fortitudo'),

(Cornish?) Oxford, Bodl. 572 ('forte').

ra, re, ri. The syllable 'pri' shews the commonest of the *r*-
symbols (p̔). Next in frequency comes 'pra,' then 'tra,' then 'gra'
and 'gre.' Occasionally 'tri' and 'cri.' All these syllables are
generally written by means of a suprascript vowel; in the case of
'pra' the *a* is often of the open form. Sometimes two commas are
substituted for the *a* in 'pra.' 'Tra' is nearly always written with
these commas; *t* with suprascript *a* is the exceptional form, e.g.
Lambeth 204. No instance of 'gra' written with suprascript *a* has
been noted; always the two commas are used for this syllable.
'Gre' is expressed by *g* with abbreviation-stroke above it; but the
inf̄ 'infra' on f. 29ʳ of Rome, Vitt. Eman., Sess. 71 should rather
be referred to the analogy of sup̄ 'supra.' Occasionally the suprascript *i* of 'pri' is replaced by a comma.

The majority of occurrences are in Insular MSS. (and Breton);
but the symbols are now current in Continental script, though
apparently not in Beneventan or Visigothic. Some examples only
need be given:

ꝓ 'pri' in Continental script: Brussels 10470-3; Leyden 88; Autun 15 and 45; Paris 1761; St Omer 765; Laon 464 and 468; Cassel theol. F 25; Cologne 53 and 113; Trèves, Stadtbibl. 169; Stuttgart H. B. VII 29; Munich 13038; Brit. Mus., Reg. 6 A v; Brit. Mus., Cotton Vesp. A VIII; Berne 87 and 128 and 167 and 172 and 207 and 292; St Gall 260; Rome, Vitt. Eman., Sess. 44; Lambeth 431 (ff. 145-160).

ꝑ with comma above, 'pri': Boulogne 90 (Anglosaxon); the Macdurnan Gospels (Irish); the Southampton Psalter (Irish); Rome, Vitt. Eman., Sess. 45.

ṭ 'tri': Brit. Mus., Reg. 6 A v; Rome, Vitt. Eman., Sess. 45.

ċ 'cri': [Oxford, Bodl., Rawl. B 502] (late Irish); the [Ricemarch Psalter] (late Welsh).

ꝓ 'pra' in Continental script: Brit. Mus., Cotton Titus D XXVII; Brussels 10470-3; Leyden 21; Autun 15; Laon 135 and 428; Paris 1761 and 3182 and 12052; Cologne 53; Düsseldorf D 1; Trèves, Dom. 136; Trèves, Stadtbibl. 169 and 170; Munich 6262 and 13038; Cambridge Ee II 4; Oxford, Bodl. 828 and Laud. lat. 26; Basel F v 33; Berne 88 and 128 and 167 and 172 and 292; Rome, Vitt. Eman., Sess. 44 and 45; Lambeth 431 (ff. 145-160). In Berne 363 (Irish) p with two commas above 'prae,' but p̄ 'pre.' In Oxford, Bodl. 572 (Cornish?) the two commas of 'pra' are joined and resemble n.

ḡ 'gre' in Continental script: Oxford, Bodl. 828 (Exeter); Rome, Vitt. Eman., Sess. 44 (Nonantola).

Two examples have been noted of an abbreviation-stroke standing for '-re' (in each case the preceding letter is e): the Macdurnan Gospels (Irish; adimplē 'adimplere'); Cambridge, Corp. Christi 153 (Welsh; docē 'docere').

In Cologne 113 'tra' is expressed by t̄a, e.g. cont̄a, t̄adunt, t̄ans. Here the abbreviation-stroke may be taken to represent suprascript r and to be the first indication of the r symbolism so characteristic of a later period.

-s. Lowe (Loew) 'Beneventan Script' (p. 213) mentions a few examples of the use of an apostrophe for final s in Beneventan MSS. as early as the first half of the eleventh century, and adds: " But the great majority belong to the second half or are later still." It really seems to be later than our period, though we noted in Rome, Vitt. Eman., Sess. 71 uniu' for 'unius'; in Manchester, Rylands 7 (of Prüm 1026–1068 A.D.) saluu', tuu', ampliu'. This same MS. uses also suprascript 's' for final 's,' e.g. 'vobĭ'; latû on f. 75ᵛ. Brit. Mus., Cotton Titus D XXVII (of "saec. xi in.") has maiu', potiu', obitu'; Lambeth 204 ("saec. x–xi") huiu', sollicitu', leviu', mortuu', inferiu', portu', Gregoriu'; and 431 (ff. 145–160) of "saec. xi," þu', reu', seriu', suaviu'.

ul. Besides the very common use of ĺ to represent medial 'ul' in all cases of 'discipulus,' 'populus,' 'saeculum,' we now find this syllable symbolized in other words, such as: oclis 'oculis' in [Cambridge, Corp. Christi 199] (late Welsh); [Oxford, Bodl., Rawl. B 502] (late Irish).

exĺtabit 'exultabit' in Rome, Vitt. Eman., Sess. 45.

singĺi 'singuli' in Berne 87 and 292 (singĺaris 'singularis').

-um. The commonest symbolism of the '-um' syllable occurs after r in such endings as '-orum,' '-arum' and (occasionally) '-urum.' Generally the symbol is formed by a vertical stroke passing through the horizontal foot of the r. All scribes employ this symbol, though it is not frequent with Insular scribes. Sometimes (as in Rome, Vitt. Eman., Sess. 44) the abbreviation-stroke is written without lifting the pen, thus producing almost a figure 8 instead of a plain stroke. The alternative form is an abbreviation-stroke above the r. This latter is mostly found in Insular script or under Insular influence. Further most scribes who write r̄ 'rum' express 'runt' by r̄t, thus avoiding confusion.

Both forms are used in such MSS. as: Leyden 67 D (under Irish influence) and 88 (from Irish exemplar); [Oxford, Bodl., Rawl. B 502] (late Irish); Oxford, Bodl. 572 (Cornish?); Brit. Mus., Add. 24142 (mostly the vertical stroke, but on f. 117ᵛ r with comma above) and Cotton Vesp. B VI; Paris 12052; Autun 45; Laon 265; Cologne 113; Trèves, Dom. 136; Rome, Vitt. Eman., Sess. 44 (only the third scribe employs the r̄-form, and he writes an s-mark in place of the horizontal stroke) and 45.

Only the r̄-form is used in such MSS. as: the Macdurnan Gospels (Irish); Cambridge Ff IV 32 (Welsh); Cambridge, Corp. Christi 153 and [199] (both Welsh); Brit. Mus., Cotton Vitell. C VIII (Anglosaxon); Lambeth 218 (Anglosaxon); St Omer 33 bis (r with comma above); Laon 468 (twice on f. 34ʳ; elsewhere r̄ denotes 'runt'); Trèves, Stadtbibl. 170 (r² 'runt'); Berne 167 (abbreviation-stroke high to right) and 207 (Fleury).

Insular examples of the vertical stroke are: Boulogne 90 (Anglosaxon); Lambeth 200 (Anglosaxon); Cambridge, Corp. Christi 307. The '-um' syllable is sometimes abbreviated after other consonants, e.g.:

ƀ '-bum' in Laon 50; Berne 207.

c̄ '-cum' in Leyden 67 D (Irish; arc̄ 'arcum'); Paris 3182 (Breton); Cambridge Ff iv 32 (Welsh); Cambridge, Corp. Christi 153 (Welsh); the [Ricemarch Psalter] (Welsh); the [Book of Deer] (Irish).

đ '-dum' in Trèves, Dom. 136; Trèves, Stadtbibl. 122; Épinal 78; Laon 428; Munich 13038; Paris 3182; Brit. Mus., Add. 11852 and Cotton Vitell. C viii; Basel B i 6 and O iv 17 (Anglosaxon). In the Macdurnan Gospels the symbol is d followed by a 7-mark.

s̄ '-sum' in [Oxford, Bodl., Rawl. B 502].

Visigothic script denotes '-mum,' '-num' by a vertical stroke through the tail of m and n (the symbols of '-mus,' '-nus' in Continental script). The Visigothic Brit. Mus., Add. 30852 substitutes a suprascript comma for the abbreviation-stroke in '-num.'

For '-tum' we find the Anglosaxon 'tur' symbol (t with vertical stroke through the right of the top branch) in the following Visigothic MSS.: Madrid, Bibl. Acad. Hist. 24 and Bibl. Nac. 10007; Manchester, Rylands 83 and 89 and 104; Brit. Mus., Add. 25600, while in Brit. Mus., Add. 30852 (also Visigothic) t² denotes '-tum.'

-unt. This syllable is most commonly abbreviated in the ending 'runt.' There are two forms, r̄t and r̄. In the latter (seldom in the former) a comma or even a 2-mark is occasionally substituted for the abbreviation-stroke. We have found no example (or hardly any) of r̄ in a purely Insular MS.; it is the Continental symbol, though in some MSS. (e.g. Beneventan) both symbols occur. Likewise the r̄t-symbol, though preponderating in Insular script (or of Insular centres), shews itself occasionally in Continental. As stated under '-um,' the r̄t-form for 'runt' occurs along with the r̄-form for 'rum.'

Examples of r̄t in Continental MSS. are: St Omer 168; Laon 97; Cologne 143; Düsseldorf D 1; Trèves, Stadtbibl. 122 and 169; Berne 292; Lambeth 237 (ff. 146–208).

Both forms (r̄ and r̄t) occur in such MSS. as: Cambridge, Corp. Christi 389 (Anglosaxon): Oxford, Bodl. 572 (Cornish?); Brit. Mus., Add. 24142 and Cotton Tib. A II (rt̄ generally, r̄ occasionally); Laon 135 (r̄ generally, r̄t occasionally) and 136 and 265 (also r with comma above); St Omer 765 (r̄t generally, but r̄ five times on f. 172ʳ); Cologne 53 (r̄t usual, r̄ rare) and 113; Épinal 78; Leyden 88; Berne 167 and 172 (also fer̄tur 'feruntur'); Basel F v 33; St Gall 46 and 90 (r with comma above); Rome, Vitt. Eman., Sess. 44 (the third scribe writes r with comma above) and 45; Manchester, Rylands 7.

The next commonest '-unt' syllable to be abbreviated is the ending 'bunt.' The usual form is b̄t, and it is generally found in Insular MSS. or MSS. under Insular influence. Examples of Continental MSS. with this symbol are: Brit. Mus., Cotton Tib. A II; St Gall 260; Berne 167 and 169; Laon 136; Oxford, Laud. lat. 26; Düsseldorf D 1; Autun 15 and 17ᴬ and 22; Trèves, Stadtbibl. 169; Munich 6262 and 13038; Rome, Vitt. Eman., Sess. 44 and 45; Manchester, Rylands 7; Lambeth 431 (ff. 145–160). The only instance of b̄ that has been noted is in Cologne 53, and here it is rare, the usual symbol being b̄t. The Beneventan [Leyden 118] sometimes substitutes a suprascript 2-mark for the abbreviation-stroke in b̄t.

Other '-unt' abbreviations are:

c̄t '-cunt' in Manchester, Rylands 7.

d̄t '-dunt' in [Cambridge, Corp. Christi 199] (Welsh); Laon 97 and 468; Rome, Vitt. Eman., Sess. 44; Manchester, Rylands 7.

ḡt '-gunt' in Frankfort, St Barthol. 32 (Anglosaxon); [Cambridge, Corp. Christi 199] (Welsh); Rome, Vitt. Eman., Sess. 45.

l̄t '-lunt' in [Cambridge, Corp. Christi 199] (Welsh; uol̄t 'volunt'), and in Lambeth 237.

n̄t '-nunt' in Oxford, Bodl. 572 (Cornish?); St Gall 260; Autun 15.

A curious abbreviation is ḡr '-gerunt' in Berne 128 ('diffugerunt,' 'coegerunt').

ur. The common and almost universal symbol for '-ur,' at least in Continental script, is now a 2-mark written above the preceding t or m. And '-tur' is more commonly abbreviated than '-mur, though of course this is in part due to the comparative rarity of

'-mur.' Examples of MSS. which use both these symbols are: Autun
15 and 17ᴬ and 22 and 31 and 45; St Omer 168 and 342bis and
765; Laon 135 and 136; Cologne 53 and 113 and 143; Düsseldorf
D 1; Brussels 1370 and 10470–3; Leyden 21 and 88 (t' corrected
to t²); Cambridge Ee ii 4; Cambridge, Corp. Christi 192; Brit.
Mus., Add. 22820 and Cotton Vesp. B vi; Berne 87 and 128
and 167 and 236 (on f. 26ᵛ t' from exemplar); Basel B i 6 (one
scribe always writes t'); St Gall 7; Rome, Vitt. Eman., Sess. 45
(on f. 48ᵛ twice m' by the first hand, m² by the second hand);
Lambeth 204 and 237 (ff. 146–208) and 427 and 431 (ff. 145–160).
These are all in Continental script. In Anglosaxon script: Cambridge, Corp. Christi 389; Boulogne 90 (the first scribe writes t'
but m²).

The occasional occurrence of the older form (t') in Leyden 88,
Basel B i 6, Rome, Vitt. Eman., Sess. 45 is probably due to Insular
influence in each case. For when we turn to Insular MSS., we find
that the older t' and m' still persist to a large extent. The 2-symbol
is unknown to such MSS. as:

(Irish) Berne 363; the Macdurnan Gospels; the Southampton
Psalter; [Oxford, Bodl., Rawl. B 502]; the [Book of Deer],

(Welsh) Cambridge Ff iv 32 (also medial 'tur,' 'gur'),

(Anglosaxon) Lambeth 218 (also medial 'tur'); Cambridge, Corp.
Christi 307 (t' and ꞇ).

We may ascribe to Insular influence the comma-mark in such
Continental MSS. as: St Gall 46; Berne 207 (Fleury; also ꞇ);
Laon 50 (sometimes altered by a corrector) and 122 (the comma
sometimes takes a 9-form) and 265; St Omer 33bis; Trèves, Dom.
136 (altered by a corrector); Trèves, Stadtbibl. 169 (the scribe
writes t² but m' which latter a corrector alters to m²).

Both forms (comma and 2-mark) appear in:

(Welsh) Cambridge, Corp. Christi 153 and [199] (t' but m²); the
[Ricemarch Psalter] (t' but m²),

(Continental) Épinal 78 (usually t² but sometimes t' and always
m'); Laon 135 and 464 (t² is normal but t' appears thrice on f. 3ʳ)
and 468 (t' t² m²); Munich 13038 (t' t² m²); Stuttgart H. B. vii
29 (t' t² m²); Rome, Vitt. Eman., Sess. 71 (t' t² m' m²).

Again it will be noticed that the MSS. which admit the comma-
form in our period are either Insular or under Insular influence.

The Anglosaxon symbol (*t* with vertical stroke through the right of the top branch) has been noted in these MSS. in Anglosaxon script: Brit. Mus., Cotton Vitell. C VIII; Valenciennes 195; Cassel theol. F 25; Frankfort, St Barthol. 32; Basel O IV 17 (also t'). Spanish MSS. do not abbreviate these syllables but employ suprascript *u* over *tr* written cursively.

The Beneventan practice is fully discussed by Lowe (Loew) 'Beneventan Script' (p. 217). In saec. viii–saec. x med. t̄. In saec. x med.–saec. xi in. t' (the comma being joined to the cross-stroke of the *t*; thus giving the appearance of a 2-mark). From saec. xi onwards t².

-us. (1) *-bus.* The commonest '-us' abbreviation is that following *b*, and the most general way of expressing '-bus' is *b* with semi-colon (b;). Beneventan examples are: Rome, Vitt. Eman., Sess. 56; Glasgow v 3. 2; Paris 335. It appears too in the [Ricemarch Psalter] (Welsh) and Leyden 67 D (with Irish abbreviation).

But there are many variants, the semi-colon being replaced by a colon, a comma, a full stop, two commas, a group of two full stops and a comma, or two commas and a full stop, or three full stops. The comma and the semi-colon are occasionally placed to the right of the *b* and above it, and quite often the two commas are written without lifting the pen in a 3-mark. The 7-shaped sign is rare; so is that like the figure 9.

In Spanish MSS. the same symbol (a suprascript *s*) is used in all the '-us' abbreviations, '-bus,' '-mus,' '-nus,' '-pus,' '-dus,' '-lus,' '-ius.' The suprascript *s* is replaced by a semi-colon placed in the same position, e.g. in Madrid, Bibl. Nac. 10007. Outside Visigothic script the different '-us' syllables may be symbolized differently.

(2) *-mus.* Next in popularity to '-bus' are the abbreviations for '-mus,' '-nus,' '-pus.' We will take '-mus' first. The commonest form is an apostrophe above the *m* (m'). Of this Insular examples are: Cambridge, Corp. Christi 307 and 389 and 153 and [199]; Lambeth 149 (ff. 1–138). Two Autun MSS., 22 and 31, use (along with m') *m* with a small suprascript *o*, so carefully written that it cannot be a mere cursive variation of the apostrophe. Other symbols are also used to express '-mus,' but frequently the apostrophe-form is found beside them. Beneventan MSS. in particular substitute the semi-colon (placed on the line) for the apostrophe. This m; appears

for example in: Glasgow v 3. 2; Rome, Vitt. Eman., Sess. 56; [Leyden 118] (along with m'). Insular scribes too have this form (m;), often with the semi-colon written cursively (mȝ). The rare 9-variety of the apostrophe appears in: Berne 292; Laon 122 and 428 (also m;).

Another form of the '-mus' syllable is fairly common, a vertical stroke through the prolonged foot of the m. When written without lifting the pen, this takes an 8-form.

Occasionally the 'mur' symbol (m^2) is used to denote '-mus.' Thus Munich 6262 has (on f. 78ʳ) m^2 'mus'; Trèves, Stadtbibl. 170 uses both m^2 and m' for 'mus,' and writes 'mur' in full; Rome, Vitt. Eman., Sess. 45 writes m^2 and m' for 'mus,' and originally had m' for 'mur' (altered by a second hand to m^2).

(3) -nus. The same symbols are used after n. Again the commonest is the apostrophe. St Omer 168 converts the apostrophe into a semi-circle (upper half) written directly over the n. One scribe of Autun 15 writes a small circle instead of the apostrophe (n°), a sign used by him also after i in the ending '-ius.' It is noticeable that the instances of m° '-mus' given above were from Autun MSS. And Boulogne 90 (Anglosaxon) writes n° '-nus.' All this would seem to shew that the o-sign is a definite form of '-us' abbreviation in our period.

Again the symbol formed by prolonging the foot of the consonant horizontally and transecting it vertically is fairly common. But n^2 has been noted only in Trèves, Stadtbibl. 170 (which occasionally shews m^2 '-mus'). The 9-form of the apostrophe too is rare, e.g. in Laon 428; Berne 108.

(4) -pus. The syllable '-pus' behaves very similarly, except that it has no symbol comparable to the vertical transection of the foot of m and n. The apostrophe (p') is quite common. Insular examples are: Lambeth 200 and 149 (ff. 1–136); Cambridge, Corp. Christi 389 and [199]; Oxford, Bodl. 572. In Trèves, Stadtbibl. 170 p' denotes the first syllable of 'possessio.'

The semi-colon symbol (p;) appears in Beneventan and Insular MSS. Examples from Continental MSS. are: St Omer 33 bis; Autun 15 (along with p'); St Gall 7 (along with p') and 260. Insular scribes affect the 3-variety of the semi-colon.

(5) -tus. The syllable '-tus' is very frequently abbreviated but

practically always by means of the apostrophe (t'). Anglosaxon examples are: Cambridge, Corp. Christi 192; Lambeth 200 and 149 (ff. 1–138); Boulogne 90 (t' 'tus' by one scribe, t' 'tur' by another). It accompanies the semi-colon symbol (t;) in Berne 128 and 172; in the Beneventan [Leyden 118]; in the Welsh Cambridge, Corp. Christi 153. But the Irish Southampton Psalter shews t; as the sole symbol. The apostrophe takes the 9-form in Laon 428; Brit. Mus., Reg. 6 A v. We will take the remaining '-us' symbols in alphabetical order: (6) -cus. First comes the usual apostrophe-symbol (c'), as in: Cambridge, Corp. Christi 389 (Anglosaxon); Brit. Mus., Add. 22820 and Cotton Vesp. B vi and Harl. 3017; Laon 97 and 136 and 468; Brussels 1370; Autun 15 and 17ᴬ; Berne 236; Manchester, Rylands 7.

Berne 292 has the 9-form of the apostrophe. The semi-colon symbol (in 3-form) occurs in the Irish Southampton Psalter and the Welsh [Cambridge, Corp. Christi 199].

(7) -dus. Cross-stroked d (đ) is the commonest form of abbreviation, as in: Basel B i 6 and B v 33; Berne 128 and 172 and 236; Paris 12296; Leyden 67 D and 88; Manchester, Rylands 7; Autun 17ᴬ and 31; Laon 135 and 428 and 464 and 468; Munich 6262; Lambeth 325; Brit. Mus., Harl. 3017 and Cotton Otho E xiii (Breton); [Leyden 118] (Beneventan). The Anglosaxon Cambridge, Corp. Christi 389 adds the apostrophe (đ'). And the semi-colon symbol (d;) appears e.g. in Laon 50 and (in the 3-form) in the Welsh [Cambridge, Corp. Christi 199]. Manchester, Rylands 98 (Italian) uses d' simply.

(8) -eus. One occurrence has been noted (e') in St Omer 33 bis.

(9) -gus. This syllable is abbreviated with the apostrophe (g') in such MSS. as: Laon 468; Basel F v 33; Rome, Vitt. Eman., Sess. 45.

(10) -ius (see under 'cuius,' 'huius,' 'eius'). This syllable is fairly often abbreviated, owing to the frequency of such words as 'cuius,' 'huius,' 'eius.' Again the universal symbol is the apostrophe. This symbol (i') denotes the first syllable of 'iustitia' in Rome, Vitt. Eman., Sess. 45, etc. Occasionally the 2-sign is substituted (i²), as in: Trèves, Stadtbibl. 170; Munich 6262 (on f. 62ʳ and f. 75ʳ; but elsewhere i'). The semi-colon form (i;) is used, e.g. in the Beneventan Rome, Vitt. Eman., Sess. 56; and (along with i') in the

Breton Brit. Mus., Cotton Otho E XIII; and in Berne 167. This
semi-colon assumes the 3-form in the Welsh [Ricemarch Psalter];
in Brit. Mus., Harl. 3017 (along with i:). The Breton Brit. Mus.,
Cotton O XIII has the colon-form in þ: 'prius.'

(11) -lus. As in the case of '-dus' the commonest symbol is cross-
stroked l (ƚ), as in: Brit. Mus., Add. 11852; Autun 45; Laon 135;
Brussels 1370; Paris 1761 and 12296; Basel B I 6 and B IV 12;
Berne 236; Rome, Vitt. Eman., Sess. 44. In Leyden 67 D (Irish)
a colon is added (ƚ:).

The apostrophe-symbol (l') occurs in St Omer 168; Brit. Mus.,
Harl. 3017 (along with ƚ) and Cotton Vesp. B VI (along with ƚ);
Manchester, Rylands 7 and 98.

The semi-colon symbol in the 3-form appears in such MSS. as:
Cambridge, Corp. Christi 389 (Anglosaxon) and [199] (Welsh).

(12) -rus. The common apostrophe-form (r') occurs in such MSS.
as: Leyden 88; Laon 97 and 136 and 468; Manchester, Rylands 7;
Lambeth 149 (ff. 1–138); Brit. Mus., Add. 22820 and Harl. 3017
and Cotton Tib. A II; Oxford, Laud. lat. 26; Brussels 1370; Berne
128; Rome, Vitt. Eman., Sess. 45. The apostrophe takes the 9-form
in Brit. Mus., Reg. 6 A v.

The semi-colon form (r;) appears, e.g. in the Beneventan [Leyden
118] (along with r'). And in the 3-form in the Irish Macdurnan
Gospels.

(13) -sus. The common form uses the apostrophe (s'), as in:
Leyden 88; Autun 22 and 45; Laon 97 and 468; Brit. Mus., Harl.
3017; Oxford, Laud. lat. 26; Berne 87 and 167; Rome, Vitt.
Eman., Sess. 45; Manchester, Rylands 7.

The semi-colon form (s;) appears, e.g. in the Beneventan Rome,
Vitt. Eman., Sess. 56, in the Irish Southampton Psalter, and in the
Welsh [Cambridge, Corp. Christi 199]. This apostrophe assumes
the 3-form in the Welsh [Ricemarch Psalter] and Cambridge, Corp.
Christi 153, and in the Irish Macdurnan Gospels (also s:).

The colon-form (s:) is used in Leyden 67 D, etc.

(14) -vus. The apostrophe-form (u') e.g. in Cologne 53 (along
with u;) and 113 (along with u;) and 143. In Cologne 113 the
9-shape of apostrophe also appears.

The semi-colon form (u;) e.g. in the Irish Berne 363 (often in
the 3-shape) and [Book of Deer] (in the 3-shape).

DESCRIPTION OF MSS.

(When the type of script is not specified it is Continental minuscule.)

AUSTRIA.

Vienna, Nationalbibliothek. 1247 Epistolae Paulinae. Written by the Irish monk, Marianus Scotus, in Continental minuscule, in the year 1079.

BELGIUM, HOLLAND.

Brussels, Bibliothèque Royale.
1370 Smaragdus; Eucherius 'Vitae SS.' From Stavelot. Datable, by a list of bishops, at 975–993.

10470-3 Prosody of Mico the Levite; Radbertus' Poems. "saec. x."

Hague, Museum Meermanno-Westreenianum. 5 Vita S.
Trudonis, etc. "saec. ix ex."

Leyden, Universiteitsbibliotheek.
21 Hegesippus. From Micy. "saec. ix post."

67 D Glossary. In Continental script, but with Irish abbreviation. "saec. x."

88 Martianus Capella. From St Pierre, Ghent. "saec. ix ex." Corrected ruthlessly by a tenth-century hand. F. 78^{r-v} is crammed with Irish abbreviation, changed by this corrector.

118 Cicero de Natura Deorum, etc. (See Plasberg's Preface to the Sijthoff facsimile.) Beneventan script. Written at Monte Cassino in the abbacy of Desiderius by six scribes, 1058–1087.

FRANCE.

Autun, Bibliothèque de la Ville
15 S. Augustini de Civitate Dei. Given by bp. Walterius (997–1023).

17^A Epistolae et Opuscula S. Hieronymi. Given by bp. Walterius (997–1023).

22 S. Gregorii Moralia. Given by bp. Walterius (997–1023).

31 (35) Flori diaconi Expositiones in divi Pauli epistolas. "saec. x."

45 (50) Rabani Mauri Expositiones librorum Regum. Given by bp. Walterius?

Boulogne, Bibliothèque Publique. 90 Amalarii Liber Officialis.
Anglosaxon script. "saec. x."

Épinal, Bibliothèque Publique. 78 Jerome on Ecclesiastes. From
Murbach. "saec. x in."

Laon, Bibliothèque de Laon.
50, 122, 136, 265, 464, 468. All given by Counts Bernard and Adelelm (847–903).

97, 135, 428. Given by bp. Dido (c. 880).

Orléans, Bibliothèque de la Ville. 79 (82) Epistolae S. Pauli. Written by Rahingus at Flavigny. "saec. ix ex."

Paris, Bibliothèque Nationale.

335 S. Pauli Epistolae. Part I "saec. ix ex."; Part II "saec. x in." Beneventan script.

1761, ff. 1–12^r Ambrose on the Epistles. "saec. ix post." The symbol mā 'misericordia' suggests North Italy as the provenience.

3182 Canons. Written by Maeloc. With Breton glosses. "saec. xi."

12052 Sacramentarium Gregorianum. Written at Corbie in the abbacy of Ratoldus (945–986). (See New Pal. Soc. II 122.)

12296 Paschasius Ratbertus super S. Matthaeum. On f. 162^r Ego In Dei Nomine Warembertus Scripsi. From Corbie. "saec. ix post."

St Omer, Bibliothèque Publique. (The MSS. come chiefly from St Bertin.)

33 bis. Theologica Varia. "saec. ix–x."

168 Gregorii Dialogi. Written in abbacy of Odbertus (987–1007).

342 bis. Évangéliaire et Passion de St Denis. Written by Dodolin (c. 993).

765 Martinellus (i.e. a collection in honour of St Martin). Given by Odbertus (987–1007).

Valenciennes, Bibliothèque Publique. 195 Alcuin. From St Amand. In Anglosaxon script. "saec. ix–x."

GERMANY.

Cassel, Landesbibliothek. Theol. F 25 Bede on Apocalypse. Written by Risalah in Anglosaxon script of Fulda. "saec. ix post."

Cologne, Dombibliothek.

53 Jerome on Prophets. Written at Cologne in time of Everger (985–999).

113 Canons. 'Liber Heriberti archiepiscopi' (999–1021).

143 Pauline Epistles. Given by Everger (985–999).

Düsseldorf, Landesbibliothek.

B 80 Gregory's Homilies. From Essen. "saec. ix–x."

D 1 Essen Sacramentary. Given by bp. Altfrid of Hildesheim to Essen (868–872).

Frankfort, St Barthol. 32 Psalter. In Anglosaxon script of Fulda. "saec. ix post."

Munich, Bayerische Staatsbibliothek.

6262 Hrabanus Maurus. Written at Freising in bishopric of Anno (854–875).

13038 Pseudo-Jerome on Pauline Epistles. From Ratisbon. "saec. ix." (See Souter 'Pelagii XIII Epp.,' pp. 286 sqq.)

Stuttgart, Würtembergische Landesbibliothek. H. B. VII 29 Gregory on Ezechiel. Written at Constance in bishopric of Eberhard I (1034–1046).

Trèves, Dombibliothek. 136 Gospels. Written by Waniggus. "saec. xi."

Trèves, Stadtbibliothek.

122 Ambrose. On f. 32ᵛ summ. by contemporary hand 'Ratpodo archieps.' (883.)

    169 Juvencus. "saec. x."

    170 Epistolae Gregorii. "saec. x."

GREAT BRITAIN.

Cambridge, University Library.

Ee ɪɪ 4 Smaragdus on Rule of St Benedict. "saec. x in."

Ff ɪᴠ 32 Juvencus. Written by Welsh scribe, Nudd. "saec. ix–x." (See Bradshaw 'Collected Papers,' p. 455.)

Ii ᴠɪ 32 The Book of Deer. In Irish script. "saec. xi." (See Pal. Soc. ɪ pls. 210–211.)

Cambridge, Corpus Christi College Library.

153 Martianus Capella. In Welsh script. "saec. ix post."

192 Amalarius De Officiis Ecclesiasticis. Written at Landevenec in Brittany in 952.

199 Augustinus De Trinitate. Written by John, bp. of St Davids, brother of bp. Ricemarch (1085–1091).

223 Prudentius. Datable by table of French kings on first page (c. 875).

272 Psalterium Achadei Comitis. Written at Rheims in 883–884. I have ignored the notes as being later than the text.

279 Canons (with Irish glosses; "saec. ix–x").

307, pt ɪ Vita S. Guthlaci. In Anglosaxon script. "saec. ix–x."

389 Vita Pauli, Vita Guthlaci. In Anglosaxon script. "saec. x."

Cambridge, St John's College Library. The Southampton Psalter. In Irish script. "saec. x–xi."

Glasgow, University (Hunterian) Library. ᴠ 3. 2. Medica varia. In Beneventan script. "saec. x in."

Lambeth, Palace Library.

The Macdurnan Gospels. Written by Maelbrigte Mac Durnan, probably at Armagh, c. 900. Irish script.

149, ff. 1–138 Beda super Apocalypsim. Anglosaxon script of "saec. x." One of Leofric's books.

204 Gregorii dialogi, etc. From Ely? "saec. x–xi."

237, ff. 146–208 Enchiridion Augustini. From Llanthony? "saec. x."

325 Ennodius. From Durham. "saec. x."

427 Psalterium glosatum Anglosax. "saec. x–xi."

431 Libellus de conflictu vitiorum et virtutum. From Llanthony. "saec. xi."

London, British Museum.

Add. 11852 Epistles, Acts, Apocalypse. Written at St Gall (before 883).

Add. 22820 Rabanus Maurus. Written at Cluny (948–994). See Pal. Soc. ɪɪ 109–110.

Add. 24142 Theodulf Bible. "saec. ix ex."

Add. 25600 Martyrology. In Visigothic script. Written for the monastery of S. Pedro de Cardeña by the scribe Gomez (919). See Pal. Soc. ɪ 95.

Add. 30852 Orationale. In Visigothic script. From Silos. "saec. ix ex."

Cotton Otho E xɪɪɪ Canones Hibernenses. Written in Brittany. "saec. x in."

Cotton Tib. A ɪɪ Gospels. Written in Germany. "saec. x in."

Cotton Titus D xxvɪɪ Offices of the Holy Cross, etc. Written at Newminster by Aelsinus for Aelfwinus (1012–1020). See Pal. Soc. ɪ 60.

Cotton Vesp. A vɪɪɪ (not ff. 37ᵛ–38ᵛ, 39ʳ–43ᵛ, which are later). Privilegium a rege Eadgaro...etc. (966). See Pal. Soc. ɪ 46–47.

Cotton Vesp. B vɪ (ff. 1–103) Baedae de Temporum Ratione. With Anglosaxon glosses of "saec. xi in." (c. 848). See Pal. Soc. ɪ 166–167.

Cotton Vitellius C vɪɪɪ Theological Extracts (ff. 86–90). In Anglosaxon script. "saec. ix ex."

Harley 3017 Miscellanea de Computo (Fleury?, 861–868).

Reg. 6 A v Fulgentius. (Lobbes, c. 1049.) See Pal. Soc. ɪ 61.

Manchester, John Rylands Library.

7 Gospel-Book. Dedicatory inscription of Abbot Ruotpertus of Prüm, 1026–1068.

83 Gregorii Moralia. In Visigothic script of 914. Written by the scribe Gomez at Cardeña. (Cf. Brit. Mus., Add. 25600 above.)

89 Cassiodorus super Psalmos. In Visigothic script of 949. From S. Pedro de Cardeña.

98 Evangelia Ottonis Imp. Written either for Otto II (955–983) or Otto III (983–1002).

104 Smaragdus. In Visigothic script of 945.

Oxford, Bodleian Library.

Bodl. 572 Varia. With apparently Cornish glosses. "saec. x."

Bodl. 828 Gospels. From Exeter. "saec. xi."

Laud. lat. 26 Gospels. "saec. x ex."

Rawl. B 502, ff. 1–12. In Irish script of c. 1100. (See Best in 'Eriu' vii 114.)

IRELAND.

Dublin, Trinity College Library. A ɪv 20 The Ricemarch Psalter. In Welsh script of 1085–1091. See Lawlor's facsimile in vols. 47–48 of the Henry Bradshaw Society.

ITALY.

Rome, Biblioteca Vittorio Emanuele.

Sessoriani 44 Jerome on Jeremiah. From Nonantola (1002–1035).

Sessoriani 45 Isidore; Remigius. From Nonantola (1002–1035).

Sessoriani 56 Gregory's Dialogues. In Beneventan script. "saec. xi."

Sessoriani 71 Jerome. From Nonantola (895–907).

SPAIN.

Madrid, Biblioteca d. Academia de la Historia.

24 Cassiani Collationes. In Visigothic script of 917. From San Millan.

25 Isidori Etymologiae. In Visigothic script of 946. From San Millan.

10067 Isidore. In Visigothic script of 915.

Madrid, Biblioteca Nacional.

10007 Vitae Patrum. In Visigothic script of 902.

SWITZERLAND.

Basel, Universitätsbibliothek.

B I 6 Fragments of Bible. From Strasbourg. Perhaps given by bp. Erkanbald (945–991).

B IV 12 Isidori Sententiae. From Strasbourg. Given by bp. Erkanbald (945–991).

F v 33 Sedulius. From Fulda. "saec. x in."

O IV 17 Sedulii Apologia. In Anglosaxon script of Fulda. "saec. ix post."

Berne, Stadtbibliothek.

87 Boethius' Geometry. Written by Constantius at Luxeuil in 1004.

88 Aratus' Phaenomena. Given by bp. Werner (1001–1029).

108, ff. 1–13 Fasti Romani. Was once part of MS. 128.

128 Orosius; Eusebius. Given by bp. Werner (1001–1029).

167 Virgil. With Breton glosses. "saec. ix–x."

169 Orosius. Given by bp. Werner (1001–1029).

172 Virgil. From Fleury. "saec. x." Written by Ildemarus, monk of Fleury.

207 Grammatici. From Fleury. "saec. ix–x." A missing part of this MS. is Paris 7520, ff. 1–24.

236 Glossary. Written by Eriulphus and Wido for Letbert in 911.

292 Varia. From Metz, c. 1060.

363 Horace, Virgil, etc. In Irish script. Probably written in North Italy by one of the Sedulius circle in 855–869.

St Gall, Stiftsbibliothek.

7 Proverbia Salomonis, etc. Written in the abbacy of Hartmut (872–883).

19 Prologus b. Hieronymi in psalterium iuxta Hebraeos. Written in the abbacy of Hartmut (872–883).

46 Ezechiel, XII Prophetae, Daniel, etc. Written in the abbacy of Hartmut (872–883).

90 Altercatio Athanasii contra Arrium, etc. Written in 869–875.

206 Beda in Actus Apostolorum, in Apocalypsin. Written in 860–867.

16904254R00053

Printed in Great Britain
by Amazon